Da√

Please return / renew by date shown.
You can renew at: **norlink.norfolk.gov.uk**
or by telephone: **0344 800 8006**
Please have your library card & PIN ready.

1	15		

NORFOLK LIBRARY
AND INFORMATION SERVICE
NORFOLK ITEM

Bloomsbury Education

An imprint of Bloomsbury Publishing Plc

50 Bedford Square
London
WC1B 3DP
UK

1385 Broadway
New York
NY 10018
USA

www.bloomsbury.com

First published 2015

British Library Cataloguing-in-Publication Data
A catalogue record for this book is available from the British Library.

ISBN: PB: 9781472913623
ePub: 9781472915979
ePDF: 9781472915986

Library of Congress Cataloguing-in-Publication Data
A catalog record for this book is available from the Library of Congress.

10 9 8 7 6 5 4 3 2 1

Typeset by Newgen Knowledge Works (P) Ltd., Chennai, India
Printed by CPI Group (UK) Ltd, Croydon, CR0 4YY

This book is produced using paper that is made from wood grown
in managed, sustainable forests. It is natural, renewable and
recyclable. The logging and manufacturing processes conform
to the environmental regulations of the country of origin.

To view more of our titles please visit www.bloomsbury.com

Contents

Acknowledgements

I'd like to say huge thanks to my family for their interest, support and in many cases, inspiration for many ideas in this book. The huge flights of fancy four young children take me on force inspiration on me with huge regularity! This book is therefore dedicated to Henry, Dylan, Daisy and Oscar. Thank you to my Mum for her constant praise and encouragement, plus her devillish first proof skills. I taught her the word tacit, which is great! She's always wanted her name in print, so Barbara, this book is also dedicated to you.

Thanks also to Ross aka @TeacherToolkit for setting me on this path, to the ever-patient Holly (First Lady of Editors) and her gentle reminders about deadlines, and Bloomsbury for having the faith to interpret 'original ideas' as a very good thing.

Max Averill coined the word 'Nextperiments' when he was in reception at the Mead School, as a way of describing what he was going to do next when he got home. This is officially **genius**, and until this portmanteau is recognised as such, I'm using this platform to share my view.

Without Twitter I'd certainly have a few more hours in my life, but be far less rich as a result. Thanks to all those brilliant Twitter Teachers for their encouragement, enthusiasm, challenge and inspiration, most especially the #goprimary collective. We may be small in number, but we do have better toys to play with than the Secondary lot!

Lastly, enormous thanks to all the teachers whose shiny new ideas I gleefully borrowed and upcycled for my own means; the schools and heads who accepted that with progress comes both risk and failure, and all the brilliant brilliant children I've taught over the years, who were swept along by the enthusiasm of a diminutive florid teacher and his fear of doing the same lesson twice, ever. You were all in my idea petri dish, and this book is a glimpse of the result; I couldn't have written this book without you all.

11:34:26   20/04/2024

Receipt for Borrow

Patron details:

Name ----------------- N * * * * * * * * * *
                              * * * * a

ID ------------------- 2 * * * * * * * * * *
                              * 8

Outstanding fees ------------- £0.00

100 ideas for primary teachers [paperback]. Outstanding teaching
Item ID: 30129076937623
Due back: 11/05/2024

Child centred planning in the early years foundation stage
Item ID: 30129086038644
Due back: 11/05/2024

The teachers' standards in the classroom
Item ID: 30129079862596
Due back: 11/05/2024

Item count: 3
Successfully borrowed: 3

Introduction

Sometimes inspiration can feel very far away when there are demands on your time, energy and mind. Almost every minute can be taken up in a teacher's day, and anything which can lighten the load can help.

Many of the ideas in this book were born from the need to think of something original and quick to implement in your classroom with a minimum of preparation and fuss. Ordinarily, you might plan a lesson with many days to prepare; turning the laminator on, downloading resources, waiting for the laminator, seeking out inspirational images to show, making a cup of tea, waiting for the laminator to reach the required temperature. However long you spend preparing lessons, there are always times when you have just five minutes to spare, if that! This then is the book for you to dip into quickly, grab an idea, twist it into your own, and launch!

Every teacher can fall into the trap of finding a good way of completing a task, delivering a unit of work, streamlining their workflow – yet despite teaching for 15 years, I'm still finding new and better ways to achieve in and out of the classroom. Dive into this book and, even if you don't think the idea will work for you/your class/your school/your dress code, see if there is something you can change in your teaching as a result (and if you can, tweet about it!).

Almost every idea in this book is a version of something else I've seen or read, or it has evolved by merging two ideas together (Scrabble + displays, the periodic table + values). Jamie Oliver once said that he didn't want people to follow his recipes word for word, but to add their own flair and twists; please be encouraged to do the same here! Every class, teacher, school and pupil is slightly different, and so some of these ideas will work far better with your class than others.

Various ideas in this book work well together, and have been loosely grouped as such, but all of the ideas will work just as well on their own. Only a few of the ideas require resources, but those that do are available in the online resources that accompany this book (see 'How to use this book'.) Look up the hashtags at the bottom of each idea and see what other teachers have come up with in their classrooms. Try to contribute your ideas online too!

I really hope this book helps inspire you, change your classroom and encourage your teaching. You spend your weekends in pound shops seeking out nifty tools for school, cut up shapes and letters until the small hours, even make giant pencils for writing displays – what makes you think you aren't *already* outstanding?!

P.S. The laminator is *almost* hot enough now.

How to use this book

This book includes quick, easy, practical ideas for you to dip in and out of, to help make your teaching outstanding.

Each idea includes:

- A catchy title, easy to refer to and share with your colleagues and Twitter peers.
- A quote from a teacher or pupil describing their experiences of the idea that follows or a problem they may have had.
- A summary of the idea in bold, making it easy to flick through the book and identify an idea you want to use at a glance.
- A step-by-step guide to implementing the idea.

Each idea also includes one or more of the following:

Teaching tip	Taking it further	Bonus idea ★
Some extra advice on how or how not to run the activity or put the strategy into practice.	Ideas and advice for how to extend the idea or develop it further.	There are 22 bonus ideas in this book that are extra exciting and extra original.

A lot of the ideas also include links to further useful resources and blogs. Online resources also accompany this book. When the link to the resource is referenced in the book, log on to www.bloomsbury. com/100ideas-primaryoutstanding to find the extra resources, catalogued under the relevant idea number.

Share how you use these ideas in the classroom and find out what other teachers have done using **#100ideas.**

Collaborative work

Part 1

Script infinitive

"Using scripts really helped to ensure the learning was secure, and demonstrated any problems in understanding too."

Asking children to explain something gives them a chance to regurgitate what they have heard, but not necessarily understood, or enables them to break an idea down into small parts. Scripts transform this process in a manner which children love and from which teachers can learn a huge amount, at every stage.

At the end of a complex concept or topic point, ask the children to pair up and write a script explaining the main points. At first, it may be simplest to ask them to write the script with three parts (two pupils and a teacher), but when they are used to this, let their imaginations run wild!

The aim may be to explain the concept, but what you are really encouraging is a written explanation, hopefully with questions or exposition from the other characters in the script. There is a discernable difference between talking about what was learned and turning this into writing, and scripts are very unthreatening tools for this.

Hover and support, and encourage the children to explain their thoughts, misconceptions and understanding as effectively as possible. In fact, mistakes should be added in, then corrected (by other characters in the script).

The final stage of this process is of course to let the children perform their scripts. Take this as an opportunity to encourage the children to reflect on each script, pulling out important features or misconceptions. Enjoy!

Taking it further

There are plenty of ways you could record these performed scripts - perhaps for your school podcast or website. You could use an app such as Puppet Pals to animate the scripts, or simply go 'old-school' and upload a video of the children performing their scripts to YouTube (check your school's policy on this first).

There are two great iPad apps which can really bring a script alive quickly: PuppetPals and Touchcast. Go to the iTunes store on your iPad and search for these apps to download them.

#scriptIt

Gamesmaker

"Originality, collaboration and such a wide variety of end results."

Board games give a lot of pleasure to groups of people, and their construction can have the same effect. Inventing board games is a really satisfying group project, where everyone's strengths can shine. Follow these guidelines over a series of sessions (potentially starting during a wet play) and create your very own games empire.

Bring into class three or four board games for children to look at, such as Pictionary, Snakes and Ladders or Monopoly. Discuss with them the basic idea of each; how the board is set out, the aim of the game, how the pieces work together and how the rules are set out.

In groups, get pupils to develop an idea for a board game. Operate the rule that if a child isn't keen on the way the game is developing, they can debate their case or join another group.

Have each group explain their game to the rest of the class and discuss what they think of the game – concept, design, name, basic rules. With any difficulties ironed out, spend a little time with each group and clarify every person's role in building the game; write these roles down on a planning sheet.

When all this has been agreed, build the gameboards, instructions and game pieces. Support the children in building their games. Give the actual boards as much attention as possible – full colour, textured backing, smooth finish, the works. The more value you give the boards, the more value the children will place on their game.

Teaching tip

A visualiser makes life easier for allowing the children to demonstrate their games – or failing that, a portable webcam.

Bonus idea ★

Ask other year groups to test out the finished games. Can they suggest improvements?

#gamesmaker

Let's get physical

"Seeing how it worked in real life made much more sense!"

We are surrounded by clever technological ways to demonstrate concepts, but nothing beats building a model or actually *becoming* what you are trying to share.

It can feel safe to have tricky concepts explained by cartoon robots or clever apps, but for real impact make these things physically. The bigger the better; they not only have a stronger impact on the school community ('What are you up to?'), but can also be easier to set up. A pyramid of brown painted boxes, complete with tissue lava and a cunningly-hidden smoke machine in the classroom, makes a striking volcano – although none of the other displays in the room will be remembered! For especially complex concepts, have the children become part of the process. The way that a motherboard works in a computer can be brought to life with some carefully-placed labels in a school hall, and children will remember this for far longer than a clever animation.

For some topics, reducing the size of the model can have an incredible impact. Teaching fractions using real pizza or, even better, cupcakes, carries the fraction message in a much more tangible way; you'll certainly never have such precisely-cut halves, and the principle of equal fractions is easy to see!

The most long-lasting impact can be when you involve the whole class in the process – make them part of whatever you are trying to explain. How often do children get to go home and say that they were the right ventricle in science that day?

Taking it further

Pinterest is an absolute treasure trove for finding really creative ideas. On Pinterest you can find collections of images, quotes and teaching ideas which you can collate into 'boards.' Use it as a search engine and see what inspiration it provides! www.pinterest.com

#getmoving

Paired responses

"Twice the brain power, and far more collaboration than normal."

This little idea really makes everyone in a pairing participate, not just the brightest or most vocal.

While I'd like to think I invented this, it is so simple that I must have picked it up from someone else (apologies if it is you; flowers and chocolates to follow).

The true power and purpose for a pairing in a lesson is not simply to hear the other person, but to allow collaboration to enhance understanding, in the way that two people solving a crossword puzzle bounce ideas off each other and, in doing so, produce inspiration that might not normally have arrived. Too often, however, it is simply an opportunity for 'talk' – things seem busy, but they often aren't particularly active.

Here, then, is the twist – when feeding back to the rest of the class, use this killer line: 'I'd like each person in the pairing to tell me what the other person said/thought/concluded'. You might want to give them an extra minute the first time you do this!

What happens when this technique is used often enough is that it forces each person in the pairing not to wait to speak (as is often the case, even as adults), but to actively listen to what the other person is saying. Encourage them to ask questions of each other – this is key to deeper understanding, and also helps them to clarify, then summarise, the other person's thoughts or answers.

Teaching tip

As well as giving pupils an extra minute the first time you do this, also help the children to summarise their points. Encourage them to turn each point into a sentence, for the other person to repeat.

Taking it further

Have two soft sponge balls, one with 'WHY' on it, and the other with 'BECAUSE'. Give them to under-enthused pairings. They have to demonstrate that they used these words in their conversations! This is explored further in Idea 20.

#pairedresponses

Logarithmic thinking

"A novel way to look back at learning in a fresh light."

Taking a different viewpoint on learning can introduce a fresh perspective for both teachers and pupils. By examining the long and short term gains of learning, children can reappraise their achievements and teachers can get a good insight into what has stuck in the children's minds.

The book *Alex's Adventures in Numberland* by Alex Bellos explains how time passes at different rates; that the details of yesterday add up to more than all the memories of last week. Our brains simply couldn't cope with remembering so much detail all the time, yet the way our children are measured expects this to be the case.

Idea 8 outlines ways to remember and recall learning and activities in the classroom, but this idea frames things in a different way. Simply make space on your board, or create a new space on your wall, and create two columns; one for last week, and one for yesterday.

At the end of each day, ask the class their outstanding (in the normal sense, not the inspection sense) memory of last week, and write this down. Next, record what their outstanding memory of yesterday was.

It is fascinating to watch this grow, and it needn't be carried out each day. In fact, try to cover up earlier answers – keep the suggestions fresh. The moments spent reflecting on the previous day and week are precious to you and your class.

#logarhythmic

Mute detective agency

"Silent fun and collaboration in one activity."

A variation on the brilliant silent debate activity, this idea encourages better mathematical explanations and collaborative problem-solving in a simple-to-organise activity.

The silent debate is a simple concept – large sheets of paper are put on group desks, and a debate ensues, using pens and comments from the (silent) children. The idea of a mute detective agency takes this one stage further, by encouraging children to solve mathematical problems and puzzles together, but silently. The benefits are huge – richer mathematical terms are used, and it also encourages the children to write down their thoughts, opinions and perspectives, which may serendipitously help another person in the group to point them towards a solution. This activity is a great way to really engage children's writing, rather than talking, skills.

It may be helpful to have some form of 'Time Out' for children to flag up if they are genuinely stuck or finding it hard to find a solution. What can be enormously beneficial is for you or your TA to pose a leading question on the piece of paper they are working on. Not only does it tick the box in terms of demonstrating your involvement, it can be a useful nudge to the children too!

The brilliant NRICH website has a plethora of mathematical puzzles, challenges and games which are perfect to use for this activity: www.nrich.org.uk

Teaching tip

This concept can be used for an awful lot more – giving directions from home to school in geography, or revising the *Wives of Windsor*, and it is a great activity to really engage their writing, rather than their talking, skills.

Taking it further

Don't reinvent the wheel - have the children create their own mute detective agency casefiles (worksheets) for next year's class!

#mutedetectiveagency

Three-legged work

"Paired work with a difference – interdependence at its best!"

Too often, paired work crashes around a teacher's ears despite the best of intentions. By considering the task from the viewpoint of a three-legged race, you can end up making much more astute choices, both in pairing and in tasks.

In a three-legged race, each person in the pairing has both a physical handicap (only one leg) and a reliance on another person (the movement of a tied leg to move forward). Move this to a paired work context and you have a clear model to use – match a weakness from each person whilst building on a strength. For example, you might match one artistic child who struggles when writing with one who has the opposite skillset. However, rather than simply asking the artistic child to do the pictures for both, they have to guide the other child, and vice versa.

The advantages of pairing in this way are numerous. As teachers, we want to encourage not only independent thinking and learning, but also knowledge of when to use expert guidance and support. In some cases this might be from teachers, but other children can also be excellent at sharing skills.

The explorer Sir Ernest Shackleton developed this system on his expeditions, constantly mixing up pairings not only to avoid cliques forming, but also to encourage each pairing to more easily recognise the talents within each other. Both these intentions are valuable in our classrooms, and with more careful planning when pairing children, both are within grasp.

#threelegged

Memory banks

"It's lovely to catch up with all we have done."

The pace of school life is incredible at times. What better than to use a few simple tools to review the year in a much simpler format than racing around at the end of the year, scrabbling to collect memories! These online tools are perfect for those moments when you are altogether as a class.

Memiary – www.memiary.com

At the end of every day, log on with your class and record five things you did/learnt/achieved. Do this over a few days and you'll end up with a bank of memories in a handy format. Quick, simple, and perfect for schools. Memiary now offers this service for pupils – what a fantastic school plenary!

Wordle – www.wordle.net

This is the grandaddy of word cloud tools. You send a link to a website, or cut and paste text (your Memiary entries) into the Wordle toolbar, and it generates a beautiful word cloud, weighting the words according to their usage. There are lots of options available (colours, fonts, directions) and images can be saved. Wordle is a great for vocabulary assessment at the end of a topic too!

Taking it further

Go offline with older children and see if they can create a word cloud of their own, with their priorities larger than other words. These are very satisfying to create!

#memorybanks

Group roles

"They began working straight away."

Group work can produce fantastic results, with careful planning and role allocation.

Much disparaged by some, we know in Primary that group work can produce pure gold. Here's how to make group work effective – assign roles.

For lots of group work, working in pairs can be sufficient, but the delay to work often comes because roles haven't been assigned – even simple things like who is the scribe, who rolls the dice, or who feeds back! Assign roles as quickly and as arbitrarily as possible. Here are three quick role-selectors:

- the youngest of the pair
- the person on the left
- the tallest of the pair.

All of these have no influence on the importance of a role, and also can't be challenged!

Although different sizes of group or role are important for different tasks, in Primary most group work is optimal at three or four participants. The key with productive work is to assign the roles as quickly as you can, with the impression of random selection if necessary. On regular tasks, it can be helpful to give out cards with role titles on them (I've used title role cards such as 'Recycling' or 'Register' with a class list, clothes pegs and class jobs successfully too). With more specific roles, it is also worth listing exactly what each person's purpose is on their role card.

#grouproles

Park the mark book

"A wrong answer tells you far more than a right answer."

In terms of efficiency, answer books and marking sheets are a gift for teachers, but there are times when they remove active thought for both the teacher and the pupil. Try these strategies to see if you can find marking more rewarding.

Do it yourself

Nothing grounds you more than completing the task yourself, whether this is a timed test or a writing task. You can feel first-hand the challenges you have set, and are also modelling your approach. I try to do this as much as possible, especially in timed tasks, as I find it keeps me on my toes. You end up with a sheet of (hopefully) correct answers in front of you, and the fear that you might (shock, horror) be wrong occasionally!

Pair and share

On a page of completed maths, one really effective strategy is to pair two completed pupils' work together, and ask them to mark it. You will find they whizz through the correct answers, but will naturally disagree over answers which are different. This process encourages them to examine and recalculate the correct answer.

Bespoke marking scheme

Tie in the children's targets with the marking and develop the occasional bespoke marking template for a task, then ask the children to self-mark. After a long time trying to solve the problem of losing my red pens all the time, my solution was to give one to every child in my class. This is a perfect chance for the children to use them.

> **Teaching tip**
>
> See if the children know what they are being marked against before they start a task. Hearing this first-hand will help to indicate their motivation! If they don't know what you are after, how will they know what to deliver?

> **Bonus idea** ★
>
> In the final few weeks before the end of the school year, mark some work from the class you are about to inherit. If you can persuade them, ask their teacher to mark some of your work. This gives you much more insight than you'd expect, and is often a welcome break!

#parkingthemarking

Focus on one thing

"No one could look away!"

In the Spanish film *Intacto* there is a scene where men are running through a forest blindfolded. It is incredibly simplistic, but also one of the most tense and gripping scenes. That amount of emotional investment, with a pay-off of learning, remains both a challenge and a goal for Primary, but it is possible; here is one example of how it can be done simply but effectively.

Teaching tip

This idea comes with a strong word of warning – you have to really know your class, and their unpredictability patterns, to try an activity like this. I'd advise against it for an observation in your NQT year, as it really could go either way – but that's part of the excitement!

Taking it further

There are many similar challenges on the internet – look up 'trust exercises' and see which are suitable for adaptation in the classroom. Bear in mind that this focus can lead to, or be interpreted as, performance. Whilst the tension is of course created, ensure that the main focus is on the learning, not the teacher!

Using a tall measuring container, discuss the scale and units on the side of the container. Agree a capacity to fill the container up to, and mark this with a board pen so it is clearly visible.

Reveal a jug filled with coloured water and a blindfold, and ask for total silence and a volunteer. It is best to choose the calmest child in your class. Ask them to hold the empty container on their head securely, William Tell style. Explain that you will blindfold yourself then pour the coloured water into the container slowly until the class tells you to stop. Any noise and you will stop pouring. Put the blindfold on and pour until the class tells you to stop.

Every time I have done this, you could hear a pin drop. The children never forget the importance of slow pouring, of accuracy, and also of your trust in them to make the right decision. It is incredibly difficult to get this level of focus on one specific skill or process, but for me, this never fails.

#keepfocused

Independent work

Part 2

Kim's game redux

"Inspiring, visual and a great way to build memorable learning."

This twist on a classic party game has real potential in class, both physically and in the way it can help to build a greater understanding of topics covered over a term in school.

In the original Kim's Game, a tray of random objects is shown, then covered, and everyone has to try and recall as many of the items as possible. In this version, the tray of objects becomes a board of learning memories, which you add to over the weeks of a term. For each session of a topic, try to find one thing you can use to represent that particular session. If you get stuck, ask the children to help you out. Add these items one by one to the board. Encourage the children to look at the items, see connections, remember the representations of the items.

In this idea, you are drawing on the children's learning memories, so this signposts what can really stand out. Encourage them to do this independently if possible (whiteboards would be perfect).

As the end of term approaches, start covering up sections of the board using banqueting roll or cloth. Encourage the children to think carefully and individually about the items on the board, and especially what they represent. This could be done with a specific representative item, or something which came up in the class discussions. I teach 'greater' and 'lesser than' using a story about pigs and crocodiles, so for this, simply having a picture of Pig Islands would be enough of a prompt.

#kimsgameredux

Explain away

"Making the implicit explicit."

Sometimes thinking aloud can be instrumental in clarifying thoughts and understanding. Explaining something verbally is excellent in helping this process to be successful.

Keep an eye out for the number of people who are talking to themselves during the day — it is far higher than you might imagine! Simply speaking aloud what is on your mind is excellent at bringing lots of thinking into one linear form. Refine and use this skill to help children make their written work clearer, and to help focus them.

Pair the children up and ask one from each pair to complete a simple task (make a chatterbox perhaps, see Idea 85). As they do this, ask the other person in the pair to talk through what their partner is doing, as precisely as they can.

Next, ask the other child in each pair to complete the task, talking aloud about what they are doing at every stage. Encourage the children to discuss the difference between the two monologues — did they use different language for example? Was it easier for them narrate someone else's instructions or their own?

'Explaining aloud' their own thought processes really can help you as a teacher to understand a child's thinking, as well as creating clarity for the children themselves. By vocalising their thoughts for an audience (their partner), this also helps to make their learning more concrete.

Taking it further

Record the monologues using mini recorders, and then allow children to listen back to them during a writing task. Alternatively, use a text-to-speech app or software to allow them to dictate directly into a computer. These are fairly accurate now, but do sometimes make mistakes, which are great to correct!

#explainaway

Roman voting

"Volvo, Video, Velcro (I came, I saw, I stuck around)."

I can't take credit for Roman voting in the least. What I do know is that it is a really simple, yet seemingly rarely-used, tool for making group decisions, while at the same time encouraging fast evaluations from your children.

A decision needs to be made quickly, such as 'Shall we go out to play?' Declare that you will take a Roman vote. After some thought, everyone votes – those who agree with their thumbs up, those who disagree with their thumbs down, and those who are happy to go with the majority with their thumbs level. At a glance, the teacher can easily see the general voting consensus and proceed.

Traditional voting systems can be very friendship-based and feudal at times, especially in the Primary classroom, with children voting based on their friends' decisions. Roman voting puts the emphasis firmly on their shoulders, and allows them to quickly form an opinion outside their influencing factors.

More importantly, the 'happy to accept the majority vote' is not uncertainty or indifference, it is an acceptance, a tolerance, that there are pros and cons to each decision which is made. As the Heath brothers wrote in their book *Decisive*, too often we tend to put every decision on an either/or basis, rather than the myriad options which there often are.

Introduce the Roman voting slowly and simply, and your class will pick up on how to use it in no time at all.

#romanvoting

Drop everything and read (DEAR)

"My favourite time of the week."

Brilliant in its simplicity, this idea creates a wholly precious moment of tranquility in a frenetic world at Primary level.

The concept here is; once a week, for 15 minutes, literally drop everything and read (DEAR). By everyone, I mean everyone, including the teacher – this is a large part of the success of DEAR. Too often, especially in the mornings, there are so many things to do that you feel more like a crisis manager than a teacher, yet the simple act of sitting and reading, alongside your class, has an amazing effect on parents and visitors to your classroom. They tend to creep in, or apologise, or even avoid entering altogether.

There is a moment where reading changes from function to absorption, and this simple 15-minute window is enough to make that magic occur. Slumped on their desks or curled up in a reading corner, the children enter a rewarding state of sustained attention.

The final, and most important, element is that the sole focus is reading for pleasure. Avoid the temptation to turn it into a reading challenge, or discuss what everyone is reading, or even have a few people read aloud. Leave it for what it is – some things are best left unturned and unbroken. Try it tomorrow. You'll love it.

Have a look at the online resources for this book for a link to a great infographic on reading.

Teaching tip

For all the activities and lessons you prepare, all the different vehicles for learning you put on, this is likely to become your favourite time of the week. You'll develop a new closeness with your class, sitting as one, being taken away to unknown places.

Taking it further

There are rumours of whole schools carrying out DEAR during the week – lock, stock and barrel, from the caretaker down! There could be no greater advocate of reading than an entire school forcing precious reading time into a filled curriculum.

#dear

Annual school retorts

"A really quick insight into how the children viewed themselves."

Use this really simple idea to gauge how the children feel they are progressing (or not) over one week at school.

Taking it further

Store these reports and give them to the relevant pupil or parent on the last day of Primary school - guaranteed to produce either tears or laughter, but possibly both!

Bonus idea ★

Some teachers find their parent meetings inevitably overrun, with or without a conversation prop such as a report. Place a watch on the table in full view. At the appropriate moment, stand up, extending your hand for a handshake and say, 'so if there are any more questions . . .' – works every single time!

The school report takes many forms, from complex letter and number schemes to pages of typed comments. Occasionally, school reports have a small box for the children to add to – what a massively missed opportunity! In every other walk of life, we would ask the person learning how they think they are getting on!

To prepare, get a copy of the school report template, and make enough copies for every child in your class. At the beginning of the week, explain that the plenary of every lesson this week will be to note down on their own school report how they think they are getting on in each subject. For each one, ask them to consider what they like, what they don't like, what they have learnt and what they need to do next to improve.

At the end of the week, read through these reports – they are fascinating and really insightful. I have used these reports with parent consultations, as they allow me to talk about how the child feels they are progressing, and I am able to contribute my perspective!

#myreport

Mastery of the universe

"If people knew how hard I worked to get my mastery, it wouldn't seem so wonderful at all." Michelangelo

The concept of mastery in the classroom, which I interpret to mean 'strength in understanding', is growing, and this view challenges the idea that simply learning what is on the curriculum is enough. Although the vast majority of focus is on becoming a subject master, why not extend this concept to those children who have mastered a certain skill instead?

I first actively recognised the benefit of this with a girl in my class who had developed certain habits which were unusual but fascinating. She always sharpened her pencil at the end of the lesson, and she never put her pencil or ruler in her pencil case. What a brilliant system! This allowed her to start working in seconds, reducing her own learning admin (see also Idea 77).

Find a child in your class who has mastered a particular skill or task which allows them to become more effective or efficient. Ask them to model this for the rest of the class, and tell the children that you'd like them to try this technique for themselves in the next few days. Examine them again and see what difference, if any, this has made.

Celebrating mastery, even of small skills, raises an unspoken expectation that we should all independently examine ways we can improve, whether learning or preparing to learn.

Share these new learning skills with the others in class and beyond, perhaps by creating a set of photographic instructions, a poster, or even giving it a branded name!

Taking it further

It takes very little time to upload a video to YouTube or Vine, so if you discover or create a little tip, share it with the world. Even better, share the video link online using Twitter or Staffrm, and don't forget to hashtag it #masterylearningtips.

Bonus idea ★

Watch this video for the most efficient way for a young child to put on a coat –it's a personal favourite (I am however biased!): vine.co/v/bU5dKBJE3Zh

#masterylearningtips

Fragments

"Incredibly diverse work from the smallest of inspirations."

Offering fragments of inspiration for the children to create around can make a huge difference to their interest and input. A little preparation makes for an incredibly rewarding task, rich with opportunities to explore planning and structure.

Teaching tip

Fragments need modelling at first, as the children will at first try to recreate what they think is missing, rather than filling in the gaps independently with their own original ideas. Model something very simply, such as the start of a familiar fairytale, or the closing paragraph of a newspaper report. The NRICH website has great story investigations you can turn into fragments.

Fragments can work with stories, artwork or even a page of problem-solving calculations. A one-page story, a long poem, a section of a playscript; even a letter or newspaper story are great to turn into fragments. Photocopy some work from previous pupils that is easy to separate into sections.

Once separated, attach each fragment to separate pieces of plain paper, so there is one fragment per page. Ensure it is in the same place as it was on the original document. The next stage is simple – ask the children to complete the work. Having a fragment of a story is both exciting and liberating, as it gives the writing some elements such as setting, character and tone, but without hugely limiting the imagination of the child themselves.

Using fragments of someone else's work encourages the children to develop more thoughtful plots (since they have to fill in details before and after a fragment), and also helps you see more clearly where the child's relative strengths and weaknesses lie.

Taking it further

Explore the diverse range of imagination within your class by giving them all the same fragment. It somehow makes a huge difference to simply using a generic story start, and the outcomes you'll get are often wildly diverse.

When using this as part of a problem-solving investigation, either use a very generic problem, or write one out yourself. Use the fragments of this for the children to rebuild their own problem to then solve – their ideas will amaze you!

#fragments

Triage

"The squeakiest wheel gets the most oil."

Triage is the skill of quickly assessing where to direct your attention, and it revolutionised medical care in the Napoleonic Wars. Take this concept into the classroom and refocus who you give most attention to in class.

Much of our role when teaching becomes tacit over time, but with this can form habits which may not be in the children's best interests.

This task is best carried out with the help of a TA. During a lesson where you are 'hostessing' (floating around the class, as opposed to working with specific individuals or groups), have them track who you help, and why, and for how long.

You will see that certain patterns are formed – very often those who are loudly requesting help are actually requesting that the teacher help them to waste some time!

At the end of this lesson, examine who you helped against the work completed. Who got your help? Can you see the impact of your help? For those you didn't assist, which children could have benefitted from your input, and why weren't they forthcoming in requesting help?

It can be all too easy to go for the noisiest children, those who are permanently by your side or whose hands are constantly up (I call them 'cloudholders'). Teaching triage helps you to identify who actually needs the active help you can give.

Teaching tip

Create a tally of the children in your class, and record every time you help them. Who do you miss out? Keep these results for the next lesson and plug those gaps!

Taking it further

There are several commercial video systems such as IRIS Connect which allow you to be record your teaching and then give you private access to the video content. This is a great way of being able to analyse where your attention is drawn.

#triage

Why/because

"Positive challenge leading to positive clarity."

The introduction of cards with 'why' and 'because' written on them can transform dialogue between a teacher and a pupil. This activity is great for developing thinking skills and enhancing inference.

Teaching tip

For older children, simply using 'why' is a superb and effective way of drilling down to intrinsic concepts in understanding. For example: 'I think Henry VIII was unhappy.' 'Why?' 'Because he married so many times.' 'Why?' 'To create an heir.' 'Why?' 'To leave a legacy.' 'Why?' 'So he wasn't forgotten.'

Make a set of cards, with WHY written on one side and BECAUSE written on the other. In a one-to-one conversation with a child where you are leading the question, hand them a card every time you say 'why' – the cards are as much a prompt for you as for them!

They then get them to hand the cards back every time they use the word 'because' – retention of the card is not an option! Encouraging the use of the word 'because', forces the children to think about their answer and justify it.

These cards are also incredibly effective in whole class teaching situations, where you can hold out the 'why' cards and give one to a child who can give you a 'because' answer. For example, you can use these cards to encourage the children to think more critically as to why the Ancient Egyptians used stone and not wood to build the pyramids, rather than simply telling them that stone was readily available and stronger.

Bonus idea ★

These cards work just as well when discussing reading, to tease out what happened in the passage previously read. Simply asking 'what has happened?' will give you a summary, whereas encouraging the use of 'because' forces the children to consider why something has happened.

#whybecause

Inquiry learning

Part 3

Stripped down speech

"Comic strips have transformed their understanding of direct speech."

Comic books and comic strips remain a much-maligned literary form in Primary classrooms. They give a tight plot and rapid dialogue in a written way which is hugely accessible to even the weakest readers, yet are seen as light literature. Using the format of comic strips, however, is a great way to get pupils engaged and to understand direct speech.

Blank or empty comic strips remain a fantastic way to encourage a much stronger and deeper understanding of direct speech. Here, 'blank' means comic strips where the speech bubbles are without any text, and 'empty' means those with completely empty bubbles and picture spaces.

Start with a simple cartoon strip (*Calvin & Hobbes* strips are three or four boxes long, and are perfect for this task) and model how to extract any direct speech, and how to turn the strip into prose.

Extend this by giving the children blank strips and asking them to create appropriate dialogue for the bubbles, then translate this into prose underneath. The children quickly see the relationship between the bubbles and the direct speech; this leads to a better understanding of speech mark use too.

In time, the children will be able to transfer speech to and from cartoon strips and text, and will understand the function of direct speech within prose.

#stripreddownspeech

Hidden learning

"Make the children think about thinking!"

Metacognition – thinking about thinking – has never been more highly rated, thanks to John Hattie's book *Visible Learning*, and the act of designing a learning tool has many valuable benefits for both the person designing the tool and the end user.

How many times have you shivered at a marketing campaign designed to be 'educational' (here's a hint, companies: wordsearches fill time, not minds), thinking that your own children could do better? Exploit this thought by setting them a learning design challenge.

Start with a very familiar concept such as road safety or swimming pool rules. Explain that they have to design an activity to help a younger class understand what they have to know about being safe near roads, and that they can use any learning format they like: a song, game, activity, puzzle, craft – the choice is wide open.

Review with them the key concepts you want to get across, making these as simple as possible, and set them to task. When they have designed their activity, get the class to review each other's work against these key concepts.

This activity makes the children think carefully about passing a message on, as well as about how that message is conveyed. It encourages the children to think about the relative strengths of different learning activities, and is also excellent fun!

Teaching tip

For some children, free choice can be just too wide and intimidating. To help them, add some restrictions to guide them to particular activities. They will still have to connect the concepts to the activity, but with less pressure.

Taking it further

Ask your class to come up with a learning design challenge for future classes. You'll be amazed with the ideas they come up with!

#hiddenlearning

Sealed moments

"This brings back the magic of post to children and teachers."

The pleasure evoked from the delivery of a letter to your own home cannot be underestimated (this is coming from someone who once spent an entire French ferry crossing filling in his name on every freepost card he could find – allegedly 21 in total)! Bring this joy into your classroom with one of these quick and easy techniques.

Post home

This takes a little preparation, but is incredibly worthwhile. Simply write a letter to each pupil, sending it to their home address a few weeks before the start of term. For a quick solution, create a photograph or postcard to send.

Send post

The delight in sending post cannot be matched. Ensure that the children have someone to write to, and get them to write a proper old-fashioned letter. The delight in this activity is in knowing that you're giving someone else pleasure in a few days time.

Mystery post

This is a charming and incredibly successful activity. Create six distinct envelopes filled with a letter, all different in style and size, and send them to your class at roughly the same time. Display each in turn and ask the children to write down what they think is inside; display their ideas around the original envelope. Obviously, you should never open the envelopes!

Taking it further

Writing letters seeking a reply can be an incredibly rewarding task. Ask the children to bring in the packaging of their favourite food products and write a letter of praise to the customer service department. More often than not, they'll get a swift and interesting response, perhaps with some vouchers included too!

#writealetter

Discover something

"Dirt and digging as a lesson? Brilliant!"

The joy of discovering something hidden or buried by someone else cannot be overstated (even as an adult!). Use geocaching to tap into those raw joys of preparing and discovering a surprise.

Geocaching is where avid cachers hide treasure boxes around the town and countryside, then leave co-ordinates and clues for others to find and exchange a small 'treasure' within. This joy of discovery transfers well to the classroom.

Ask the children to bring in something inexpensive but precious to them. Beg them not to reveal it to anyone else, and if they can wrap it up in kitchen roll and then in a sandwich bag, so much the better (as the prep is then done for you).

Have the children write down what the object means to them, but without explicitly saying what it is. Keep these sections of writing ready for after the main activity.

Take the children outside with trowels and lolly sticks, and find an area of ground you can bury these treasures. Use the lolly sticks to mark the items.

After a few days, take the children back outside and have them dig up the treasure beneath a different lollipop to their own. Then ask them to write about why the item might be precious to someone.

Finally, try to match statements to items. Let the children discuss, debate and discover new things about each other; have them read new writing with fresh eyes.

Teaching tip

Some items will be harder to write about than others, so be on hand to help. Mark your burial ground with something quite permanent to ensure you don't forget where it is, and ensure you seal your container well (twice even) to avoid anything perishing.

#discoversomething

Objective duct tape

"Sticky learning made physical!"

Curiously, few things get Primary SLTs more excitable than their desire to see learning objectives on the board for every lesson. Some even see the benefit in children writing these objectives into their books, which is not a particularly valuable use of learning time in schools. For those who'd rather have the children learn something than copy something from the board, here are a few ways to leap this particular learning hole.

Objective strips

Type out the learning objective, looping each end, so that

RECOGNISE VERTICES IN 2D SHAPES

becomes

IN 2D SHAPES RECOGNISE VERTICES IN 2D SHAPES RECOGNISE

Repeat this line over and over on one page, then cut out the lines. Give them to the children to trim correctly then stick in their books. For older children, add some random words for them to delete as appropriate; this will help them to focus on what their actual objective is!

Objective texts

Put a letter limit on the board, and tell the children the objective of the lesson. Can they summarise this into a word or phrase below the word limit?

Sticky labels

For an even more efficient system, use the address label templates that come preloaded with Microsoft Word, together with sheets of white sticky labels, to print out objectives en masse.

Title it

Make the title of your work the objective if possible – this kills two birds with one stone! Putting this on the board alongside the date and asking the children to write it into their books at the start of the lesson ensures that they can begin any task straight away.

Post-it timetable

A good rule of thumb for objectives is that if it can't be written on one Post-it note with a felt-tip pen, it is too long! Test this out by measuring a standard Post-it note, and building a paper display of your timetable around this. Write out the objective for each lesson on the Post-it for that lesson space. If it needs more space, shorten it!

Objective swaps

Have an older class visit you with three objectives written up. Have those children show your class their work and see if your class think that they match up correctly. Be careful who you ask to do this idea with – nothing makes a teacher sweat more than another class judging their work!

Objective snips

One brilliant idea is to cut up the words of the objectives and put them in an envelope. Children then have to open the envelope, sort the words and solve what the objective of the lesson was – what an excellent starter!

Taking it further

Use a coloured highlighter to indicate the learning objectives in the children's books. Perhaps consider using different colours to show understanding – green for objective understood, yellow for partial understanding, pink for none.

Bonus idea ★

Create a Wordle (word cloud) of your objectives for one week, photocopy this, and get the children to highlight/colour in ones they feel are most secure.

#pimpmyobjectives

The hard sell

"Persuasive writing has never been more fun!"

The hard sell takes inspiration from pitching competitions such as Startup Weekend and *Dragon's Den*. A mix of advertising, promotion, scrutiny and debate, the children invent problem-solving devices and then pitch these to an audience.

Start by brainstorming everyday problems which the children may face. Ideas could include:

- keeping sandwiches cold
- sharing out sweets without touching them
- rubbing things out without leaving rubber dandruff.

Create some inventive solutions or products that solve one or two of these problems (the sites in the links below can give some inspiration), and show how you might write a speech to model this problem and solution in under a minute – around 150 words – in a *Dragon's Den* style pitch.

Set the children the challenge of creating their own product which solves a problem. Get them to create a pitch script and a design picture, and also have a robust defence of their idea. At pitching time, give each child one minute for their pitch presentation, allowing time for a few questions afterwards, and stick their designs up around the classroom at head height.

When all the pitches are finished, give each child three Post-its – these work as votes which they stick under their three favourite designs. The one with the most votes wins! This activity unleashes a new level of creativity with the children, whilst encouraging them to develop strong persuasive skills (and hear some great ones too).

#hardsell

Match the fact

"Everyone wanted to answer, but nobody knew the question!"

This is a great way to introduce a concept or objective without doing it explicitly. There is a lot of contention over discovery learning, but this activity perfectly demonstrates how an effective hook to introduce a lesson concept can also work in encouraging challenge and curiosity in children.

This idea uses geography as a theme, but this type of activity is easily adapted – you could have a passage of text on the board, or five different sums.

Objective: Recognise that countries can be bordered by water, other countries or both, and how this can affect them in a variety of ways (Year 4).

Put a map of Europe on the screen; remove country names for an extra challenge. Tell the children that they can name a country and you will respond with a number. The children simply have to work out the connection between the country and the number. You will find that they get the idea immediately and start naming countries – tell them the number of countries which border the named one.

You will see the children start strategising, and eventually they will start guessing the connection. At this point, introduce the rule that you can't guess the rule, but you can give a country and the number, and test your prediction.

This lesson starter provokes an enormous energy level, which will remain throughout the lesson. By capturing their interest, you will lead the children toward an objective which could otherwise be very dry.

Teaching tip

Let your TA know your intentions beforehand so that they can help steer the thinking where necessary.

Taking it further

Some activities lend themselves to this type of introduction better than others – but ask the children if they think you could have introduced something more effectively. They can be our harshest critics but best guides.

#hiddenlearning

31

Fictional families

"It was great to see the children building up the family tree as the story continued."

We can often see the connections in a story quite easily, whereas for children they might not be so apparent. Building family trees for fictional characters helps the children to see the connections between the people in the story.

It is worth introducing a very simple family tree to the class before embarking on this activity so that they understand the basic format. You might also want to sketch out a familiar family tree from a previous book in order to show one being built.

Dedicate some space to this tree at a focal point in the classroom, and create the tree as you read the story. Take this opportunity to explore the different relationships, and how the dynamics work together. For example, in *Danny, the Champion of the World*, although there are only two main characters, there is a larger supporting cast you could build into the family tree.

Creating a family tree is an excellent way of building deeper understanding of a text. It can help to make sense of decisions, conflicts and challenges which the characters face during the course of the story, and can also assist in understanding the plot with greater clarity.

Taking it further

Have the children create a fictional family tree and then build a story plot from the tree. Name dictionaries are brilliant resources for seeing what name would suit certain characters.

#fictionalfamilies

Magnified introductions

"Building up a bigger picture, literally."

The tale of the Blind Indians and the Elephant, where each blind Indian feels a different part of an elephant and concludes it is different to all the others, illustrates how multiple opinions can bring a new perspective. This can be put to exceptionally good use with the magnifying glass technique, which creates a new viewpoint on the topics covered.

In its simplest form, find a specific and relevant picture related to the topic you are studying then cut it into sections, giving each child/group a section, and asking them to make predictions about what you are exploring in that session, or what they think is going on.

Since the children will all have different sections of the picture, they will all bring a different perspective. Really effective image choices will not only bring out interesting predictions, but will also encourage the children to draw on previous knowledge and experience. Fire insurance shields, which were put on buildings in Tudor times to indicate to private fire services who had or hadn't paid in case of an accident, are perfect for an introduction into either Tudors or Homes, and an image of a shield can be found very quickly online.

These snippets of images can also operate as a good writing stimulus (see Idea 35 Fear of the blank page) as well as a learning memento for books.

Teaching tip

If you have not heard of the tale of the Blind Indians and the Elephant, do look it up – search 'Blind men and an elephant' in Wikipedia for an overview.

Taking it further

The more technical among you may want to use a presentation program to display a picture and, using animated shapes, unveil the image section by section, building the dialogue with the class and creating the picture as you continue.

#magnifiedintros

Playground survival

"Makes standing in the cold feel like a wasted opportunity."

Who doesn't like a little bit of people-watching? All human life is on display in the Primary playground, yet it is the dip in some teacher's days. Also, as any Primary teacher knows, a problem in the playground can potentially ruin that well-planned lesson. Here are some tips to making it a far better and more survivable experience – for everyone!

Draw the play web

Choose a child and track their play during break time. How many children do they interact with, or come into contact with? Who is leading their game? Is there just one game or are several going on at the same time? This focus on one child or group of children is really interesting, and by building their play web in your mind (their friendship groups and interactions), you gain a much stronger picture of their sociability dynamic.

Big letters

If you get really bored on playground duty, imagine the whole space and spell out your name, one giant letter at a time. This is great for making you walk around in a different way, and getting to see different groups playing together. It also stops you remaining static and getting cold!

Equipment rotation

New equipment is put outside and is used endlessly until it wears out. But why not simply have a box of activities for each day of the week? Each box contains a themed set of resources (throwing, skipping, hoops, paired, high/low) to be used once a week. These resources last five times longer and the interest of the games is extended.

Taking it further

Revisit the playground rules often – what the children raise during the year reflect the evolving culture of what is going on outside.

#playgroundsurvival

Developing mindsets

Part 4

One ambitious target

"It's my goal, but we all know what I'm aiming for."

We keep a myriad of data on children, including a range of targets. If we find these hard to manage, why do we expect the children to juggle all their targets in their heads? Take these steps to trim woolly targets into something more meaningful and achievable for you and the children.

Targets are too often hidden away, pinned on boards, or stuck inside books. How can this help as a focus for a child? A good target needs to be a mantra, a thread running through all their work (both interactive and written down).

Pare your children's individual targets down into a big, visionary mantra. Make it big, bold and visual – 'to become a better writer' doesn't have the impact of 'to take my readers on a journey like Michael Morpurgo'. Have a mantra of your own (mine is, and remains, 'get tidier in hand, heart and mind'!) and develop opportunities for everyone to share their mantra whenever possible. Responding to registration names (see Idea 53) is one way, but it also can be something repeated while lining up for lunch, or before home time.

Help children achieve their mantras. Ask what the child can do to ensure that their contributions and work help to develop their mantra. These will genuinely engage the class in a way you might not have predicted; in a supported environment, children will start helping each other to achieve their one ambitious target.

Teaching tip

The sneaky aspect is that mantras are incredibly easy to work toward but incredibly hard to complete or sign off (see my tidiness mantra!) so they can last all year.

Bonus idea ★

Build a paper chain of achievements for your class, adding a link every time they shine as a class, ready to review at the end of the year as a celebration. This lends itself well to a perfect, incredibly-easy-to-prepare class assembly for the end of the year.

#oneambitioustarget

Learning Lent

"Giving myself a restriction has forced me to be more creative."

Breaking long-established patterns of habit can be a great tool to discover improved ways to help teaching and learning.

Why do people stick with defaults, for example, using Times New Roman font when there is a near-limitless range of fonts online? Given the enormous range of choices we have these days, it seems strange to simply let someone else make this choice for you.

Instead, try a Learning Lent. This is when you give up a default for a fixed period of time (anything from one week to half a term), and see what emerges. Perhaps the easiest default to change is to try not to give the children anything on A4 paper. Play with sizes; experiment with colours, shapes, blocks and strips.

It is important to note that what you try instead may not necessarily be better; the real purpose is to explicitly examine your default choices in a new light. Restrictions force you to think creatively, to improvise, to re-examine a problem from another angle – it is this challenge that makes a Learning Lent so beneficial.

Try choosing one of these Learning Lents:

- No photocopying
- Only colours, no black or blue
- No A4
- No internet
- Outside
- No writing
- Relate to news headlines
- No sitting down
- No desks
- No interactive whiteboard.

Taking it further

I have long harboured a dream to wrap up the school photocopier in clingfilm and see what impact this has on creativity. What other major tool do you now use blindly which would force you to adapt your practice?

Bonus idea ★

Schools which have been victims of arson often have an enforced Learning Lent. How would you manage and what would you change if your classroom was half the size, or based in a corridor, or even outside? What could you take from this and introduce into your current classroom?

#learninglent

Three-minute clinic

"Appointments are fast and the diagnosis is good!"

Try this rapid turnover way for getting superb input and feedback during a depth task. Not only do you get to see and mark all work, the children get some exclusive use of the best learning resource you can offer — your feedback!

We all remember the lovely indulgence of our teachers making time just for us, yet it can be a real challenge to make this a reality. Next time you run a depth task (long, sustained, perhaps over several lessons), try a three-minute clinic.

Using an egg timer or equivalent, set the timer for three minutes and invite children up to your desk to have active written feedback. You should ideally sit next to each other and narrate what you are doing as you mark, with the child free to ask questions as and when they want to.

The children genuinely love this, as they can see your marking and hear your positive feedback. You get a really thorough chance to fillet one piece of work (plus reduce your marking), and the children become accustomed to the speed benefits of a clinic.

Taking it further

Why not have the next child sitting on the other side of you, listening to the feedback you are giving? It only costs another three minutes, and they are likely to get some benefit too. It is also worth dating their books so you can keep track of who has attended a clinic!

#threeminuteclinic

Broccoli sentences

"Four sentences in one, and a massive sense of achievement to boot!"

Broccoli sentences are a way to shake free of the stand-by 'Write ten sentences using x'. While there are benefits to these exercises, too often the emphasis is on the content rather than an effective use of the type of word or function you are teaching, such as adverbial phrases or subclauses.

Ask the children to mark a small dot in the margin of their books every five lines and tell them that this is the start of their sentence. These are best to demonstrate first and follow a fixed format of sentence, with the first 'branch' in the first part of the sentence, and a second 'branch' from each of these. In the example below, the focus is on adverbs.

The boys ran — noisily down the corridor — in order to avoid the alarms.
                 — through the muddy field — so the dogs didn't catch them.

Splitting a sentence into four parts allows the children to really exercise their use of the focus (the adverb), and also how that focus can take different directions. Too often, the start of a sentence is the challenge for pupils, whereas the end tends to write itself. Broccoli writing has a bland, generic start, and the creativity propels the writing forward.

Another huge advantage over the ten sentences approach is that the children can quickly fill a page, and the layout feels less onerous than conventional sentence tasks.

Taking if further

Broccoli sentences lend themselves quite neatly to choose-your-own-adventure stories. Get more able children to number the ends of their sentences to create a narrative with them.

#broccolisentences

Fear of the blank page

"By adding more to the page, the quantity, and quality, of writing actually increased!"

When it comes to extended writing, there are three camps — those who are itching to start straight away, quickly filling a page with writing seemingly with ease; those who slowly work their way down a page, occasionally increasing or decreasing in speed; and those poor souls who look at the blank page sitting there, waiting to be filled.

Teaching tip

Keep your eyes peeled for unusual images and headlines, and collate these online using tools such as Pinterest or Flickr. Even better, have a small folder of them near your desk to use as 999 stimuli!

We have all been there, whether it is filling in a passport application form or composing an awkward letter. The pressure of completion is immense, and for some children this induces a feeling best described by the sporting term 'choke', where they don't feel they can carry on, or even begin (Matthew Syed's book *Bounce* explores this in more detail).

There are several steps you can take to reduce this anxiety, whilst at the same time increasing the quality and quantity produced by the children. One of the most successful strategies is to have a visual stimulus either pre-stuck onto the page or given out and stuck on by the children themselves.

Try using the funny Dinovember series of pictures (see link on page 41). Give the children a choice of pictures to use as a writing stimulus, all printed to A6 size — that way the children can stick them in the top-left section of their A4 lined books. Instantly the pressure to fill a page is decreased by 25%!

Writing in the space to the side of the picture is also less threatening, and it can be filled quite quickly. The advantage of this strategy is that it doesn't restrict the more confident writers, but does support the less confident.

The other mainstay technique is the prompt strip – a coloured strip with some simple reminders laid out on it, glued into the side of the book past the margin, which reduces the page size while giving handy and constant prompts. Try using coloured paper – it really does make a difference (and since you can get four strips from one A4 piece of paper, is environmentally friendly too).

Headlines

A set of lovely, bold and unusual headlines stuck into the top of a book can take up space as well as providing a fantastic stimulus for some creative writing. With a little careful thought, they can also be really simply differentiated, so the children who have 'The Fear' have a headline with more words; the turbo writers far less.

Disconnected

Two small pictures, stuck in diagonal corners of a blank page take up space and provide a great stimulus, the lower picture providing the 'target' a piece of writing is heading toward. To make it even more of a challenge, choose pictures with no apparent connection to each other!

Links

The cc search is a brilliant search engine for school-friendly copyrighted images: creativecommons.org

Dinovember is a clever idea in pictures: dinovember.tumblr.com

Taking it further

There are several websites which have royalty-free images of unusual paper. Old lined paper, faded maps and yellowed sheets are all readily available, and look impressive when stuck into a lined book, as well as matching a genre more successfully!

#fearoftheblankpage

Microticks

"Microticks allow every child to feel success."

Microticks are great fun to operate within the classroom, and children find them incredibly rewarding to collect and draw. Put simply, you extend the criteria for success in any task, and make the task more than simply getting the right answer.

A microtick is a full tick broken down into smaller parts, rewarding each stage of an answer. In teaching column addition, for example, explain to the children about to mark each other's work that each question is worth three microticks; one for numbers in boxes, another for having two parallel answer lines and a third for the right answer. Using microticks makes a ten question page of problems worth 30 marks, and highlights to the children your particular focus with the task in hand.

Children enjoy marking each other's work; operate a 'random swap' for books – sometimes swapping two or three times. Use coloured pencils to mark, to avoid any temptation to adjust any answer. The microticks are small and strong; you should also ask the children to give a total mark, and an encouraging comment. You'll be overwhelmed by the thought that children put into this, and might find yourself borrowing their inventive phrases!

It is important to remember that if the focus of the lesson is to answer the questions correctly, your assessment should feed into this. Microticks allow everyone to achieve, as well as emphasising things that might have been in decline over the course of the lesson.

Hivemind agony aunt

"A problem shared is a problem out in the open."

Why do we not use the experts in our own classrooms? (Hint: They sit in front of you every day.) We are more than capable of solving problems which aren't about ourselves with ease, yet often choke when the same dilemma is our own. The following task aims to reverse this completely.

Explain a problem you have with class admin, organisation or tidiness; something very real and tangible. Have the class discuss it and come up with possible solutions to the problem. List these on the board, then categorise them as numbered solutions to try (or dismiss). Indicate the ones you would have thought of, and celebrate new ones from the children which didn't occur to you.

Now it is the turn of the children! Ask them to think of a similar problem they may have (avoiding anything personal). You may choose to either have papers passed around for the children to add their solutions to, or stick the problems around the classroom to create some energy, flow and movement. Either way, encourage the children to contribute to each problem with solutions that are as interesting as possible.

You'll end up with a wide variety of ideas and possible solutions for the children to try, as well as some yourself. The children will also have had a chance to really celebrate their expertise! This activity can also provide valuable content for a circle time with your class. I once did this with my children, and they gave such moral answers I suggested I email their parents to confirm this was really the case!

Taking it further

Review the solutions after a few weeks. Which worked best? Which could be shared with others? Which could be adjusted for other children?

#agonyaunt

Permission to forget

"Realising there is too much to remember gave me the freedom to forget some things."

We can overwhelm our children with knowledge, stimulation and information, encouraging them to gorge until there is little pleasure left. There are some children who thrive on knowledge like this, but for many others something has to give. How often do we give children permission to forget?

Trying to remember what has been covered is incredibly important (as Idea 8 shows), but so too is the allowance we give for the children to forget things. Just as adults find it incredibly hard to recall facts, details, dates and names, so do children.

Giving your class explicit permission to forget may seem daft, but it recognises that they aren't vessels to be filled. This is done through a culture of acceptance that we are all fallible. Here are some phrases to pepper into your class talk:

- 'What was important that we will probably forget?'
- 'If we don't remember all of this, how could we relearn it in the future?'
- 'I don't expect you to remember all this – what would you say are the key parts?'

Improving or refining memory skills are of course incredibly important, but it is far more crucial that the learning journey continues, with the skilful picking of the right things to remember. Make your own confession to the class: 'I've taught Henry VIII five times. Every single time I have to relearn the facts. It just doesn't stick!'

#permissiontoforget

Scorify

"Scorifying made me really proud of my work."

The concept of gamification is becoming more and more popular in schools, and in the EdTech sector in particular, but the danger it produces is that children compete for the score reward rather than the achievement of learning itself. We want to appreciate the hoops rather than just jumping through them. Scorifying challenges this head-on.

The power of feedback, both constructive and immediate, is celebrated as one of the most beneficial forces in improving learning, and Scorifying some completed work is great for building active dialogue (as opposed to simply pat answers) in the style of a university viva.

When working with your children one-to-one (see Idea 33, Three-minute clinics), ask them to score their work. Allow them to set their upper limit, and then ask them to justify their score. This will encourage them to consider their work afresh, and by considering a score they are also evaluating their work against a new criteria – their own.

You needn't record this score; the aim is to open up dialogue in a way that comparing against objectives or a set marking scheme doesn't. It is interesting to ask the children what they could do to improve this score. You will see from their answers exactly what they believe would improve their work; it will not necessarily be what you would do. Use this rich dialogue to support their learning and Scorify. Used sparingly, it can prove to be a really neat way of accessing an internal criteria.

Teaching tip

Use their ideas to improve as key aspects to your comments when marking, using underlining or speech marks to highlight they've been part of the process.

Taking it further

Encourage the children to share their scores with each other. Better yet, have them score each other's work.

#scorify

Award ceremony

"Exciting, touching and incredibly rewarding."

If you have tried Good deeds (Idea 56), you'll really appreciate the pleasure a customised awards ceremony gives to the children. Not only does this task encourage the children to think with renewed care about one specific person in the class, it also encourages writing with depth.

Teaching tip

This is a perfect task to schedule at the end of the year, when work is much harder to carry out. This is especially significant for Year 6 pupils. Expect tears! Why not have the Head present a few at the end of the school disco, with childhood pictures of classmates on the big screen in the background?

Model an award (this is a great chance to praise your hardworking TA!) by giving a small speech about how great the receiver is. Try and make this as specific as possible, focusing on one attribute or feature. For example:

'We all know Chloe has some fantastic ideas when she is writing stories. More importantly, she isn't precious about sharing her ideas with others, and she is always helping us out in class by putting her hand up, coming up with clever situations or characters, and letting us all take these ideas and put them into our own work. Thank you Chloe for your unending generosity!'

Write the children's names on pieces of paper, and distribute these secretly, so they don't know who has their name. The task is to write an award speech for that person. Ideally they would write about a particular skill or attribute, but for some children (and award subjects) it may be easier to write in more general terms.

Carry out an awards ceremony. Have a small token award to present, and ask each child to make their speech and present their award. The quickest but perhaps least permanent award you can give is a cardboard thumbs up, taped to a lolly stick, and poked into half a potato, all sprayed in gold paint. Although this sounds naff, it costs pennies and is incredibly fun!

#awardceremony

Grit and flow

Part 5

Inspiration station

"These ideas made creative work flow much more easily!"

While some children can find inspiration in the smallest, and most unlikely, of places, others have a definite block when it comes to being actively creative. Here are some tips for introducing creative methods and ideas to your classroom.

Teaching tip

Panic trays are great for children who 'get stuck' but are actually trying to kill some time. These are trays filled with interesting images, objects and 'stuff'. Ask the child to choose two items at random from the tray and include these two items in the next five sentences they write.

Visuawall

Challenge the children to each find one striking image; add the images to an A1-sized board as they are given to you, and use them as a prompt for creative work in the classroom. Ask those who are especially creative to choose two images and connect them in a story.

Flickr interestingness

The Flickr photo sharing website has a section called Interestingness: www.flickr.com/explore/interesting, which is filled daily with really striking images, many which are copyright-friendly for schools. Due to the nature of some of the images, it may be advisable to browse through them beforehand! Print and laminate these for some quickfire stimulation, or store links to them to start each day.

Random articles

Wikipedia is a brilliant resource for schools, and on the main home page is a little-known feature called 'Random Article' en.wikipedia.org/wiki/Special:Random – click this to get something from the archives. This can give you a whole range of ideas for themes, settings and characters; even topics for debate! You could use it to create band names when designing CDs in computing lessons.

Oddjects

We are all drawn to the unusual, and this can be a rich seam of dialogue for the children and you when seeking inspiration. Trawl bric-a-brac and boot sales for unusual items to keep in a box or on the shelf in your classroom. I'm currently fascinated by the old glass green bottles – one with a cork could be a secret potion, a hideaway for fairies or the vessel for a message in a bottle.

Up close

You occasionally find pictures in newspapers or online of ordinary items taken with a macro camera, so it is if you are looking under a microscope – even the most mundane items are often very hard to identify! Collate these images as you see them, and ask the children to find inspiration in what they imagine they could be photographs of!

Paint colours

The imaginations of the people who invent names for different shades of paint know no bounds, and the popular DIY warehouses often have a range of catalogues and card strips with colours and their associated names. As a way of encouraging creative thinking, why not cut these up and ask the children what they think the names could be – a new invention, a planet, a disease? The wonderful and addictive Pinterest website has a plethora of creative ways to use the paint card strips. Type in 'paint sample crafts' and let your imagination run riot!

Taking it further

Fridge magnets are available which have a range of words on them, allowing you to create silly sentences with them – genius. Have these along the bottom of your board, and choose two or three at random which must be included in that day's writing. Once used, return them to the bottom, but turned upside down so that they avoid being selected next time.

#inpirationstation

Propp up your characters

"Suddenly plots became really clear to understand."

In 1928, Vladimir Propp published *Morphology of the Folktale*, which was incredibly influential in unpicking the central core of a story. He analysed over 100 Russian folk stories, and, in doing so, identified 31 basic plot developments and seven key characters in any story.

Teaching tip

You may well find it helpful to remind the children of the different characters if they get stuck when writing a story. 'Do you have a false hero? What might a messenger bring? Who is the real hero, and how do we know?' are all fantastic starting points to nudge more writing.

Taking it further

Type up the character traits and pass them around the class seven times, adding a name to each of the types. You instantly have 30 characters without a story – perfect for launching some creative ideas from the more reticent!

If you are working on characters, stories or plot, an understanding of these seven characters can be immensely powerful in terms of allowing the children a deeper comprehension of how a plot actually works. The characters are as follows:

- hero
- princess
- villain
- helper
- donor
- messenger
- false hero.

(Note, some of these may be shared roles.)

Using a well-known story or film to initially understand the different roles is essential. *Finding Nemo* is excellent, as is *Charlie and the Chocolate Factory*. Write down the character types, and work out with the class who is who in the film or book.

Return to these types again and again. You will find that the children will begin to identify the characters in their books, stories, even the films they see at the weekend! The benefit this brings is in understanding the purpose and motivation behind the characters in a story.

#proppthemup

Teacher bound

"Letting go was hard at first, then liberating! I could feel the quality of my dialogue with the children improving instantly."

Some teachers intervene in children's learning far more than is sometimes necessary, and this idea is a small, slightly bizarre, way to try and curb unneeded interruptions.

One mainstay in lessons, particularly when the children are having to explain something, on the board is to tell them to pretend they are answering you on the phone. This forces them to use a more descriptive language in their response, as well as avoiding them using a pointed finger to the notes on board by way of an explanation.

Take two flesh-coloured elastic bands and put them around your fingers at the knuckle joints. This is to remind you (physically and visually) to keep your hands away from the children's work. This is especially key on practical tasks such as artwork, craft, construction, science experiments and computer work. The desire to dive in and show them/take over may feel overwhelming, yet by restricting yourself you will find that your dialogue with the children becomes so much more refined. You'll use more clear instruction, describe things more effectively and allow the child to learn by doing, rather than by seeing and having done for them.

The aim is to prevent teacher modelling becoming teacher doing. By restricting yourself from getting involved, you are making tacit decisions about how best to assist and progress the learning on their behalf.

Taking it further

Ask a TA to carry out an informal work study, and let you know in which subject you tend to be more hands on than others. You'll be surprised.

#teacherbound

Time chasing

"This made my class work at speed, and the work was good too!"

The speed a class works at can vary in pace — below are three small tips to either maintain or increase your pace. A word of warning: more work doesn't always equate to better work. Using these tips sparingly demonstrates grit in a really effective way, as it takes the focus off the work and onto keeping to time. All examples use extended writing as the task in hand.

Teaching tip

Where are the clocks in your classroom? Check now! Ideally there should be one for you, and one for the children, each in the directions you face. I was given a backwards clock a few years back, and this regularly confounds adults!

Time is one of the most precious commodities in a Primary school (after Blu-Tack, obviously), and all too often teachers have to play a balancing act between finding time to fit objectives and topics in, and losing time with interruptions. Perhaps one of the biggest ironies is that the 20 minute tea break feels like two minutes, and the 20 minute playground duty feels four times as long (see Idea 30 for help here). Also amazing are the children who find reading the time hard work, but know exactly what time lunch is!

One of you . . .

This uses something known as spindle theory, which is that people working together are generally more productive than those who work on their own. This works particularly well with talkative groups of children.

Put a coloured dot after the last word on everyone's page. Tell the children that you are tracking one child on the table to see how much he or she writes in the next seven minutes. You will notice an immediate change in tempo! The best part is that you can look at everyone's work after seven minutes and not even announce who you were supposedly watching in the first place.

Margin times

This works brilliantly when working one-to-one with children who work well with personal bests and challenges (so is perfect for homework, parents). You simply write the time in the margin for every new line. Start off by writing it for the children, and they'll soon get the incentive ('I only took two minutes to write that line') and log the time themselves. This works particularly well with reluctant writers.

I first discovered the benefit of this when trying to incentivise my eldest son into completing some homework. He is training, like his father, to become a professional procrastinator, and will make a 20 minute task last two hours! By seeing how quickly he was completing each sentence, he became instantly motivated to beat his time! WIN!

Dot the minute

This is extreme, but works brilliantly as a boost for a lesson whose pace has begun to flag. Ask each child to get out a coloured pencil, and then ask them to put a dot above the word they are currently writing, every minute. Have them do this for ten minutes and then reflect on their pace. Did they get faster? Did their work rate improve?

Taking it further

There is a common trait in many of the teachers I admire, and that is that they almost all use music to encourage completion/tidying up/the end of the day. I love this, and try to do the same when I'm with my class. It works wonders as it can lift the spirits of the class, and if familiar to them, they'll know the timing of the song too.

#timechasing

180-degree writing

"Amazing work and deeper understanding in one hit."

This idea works as a neat introduction to changing perspectives, but can also secure better comprehension when carried out in English.

Teaching tip

To find the writing voice, select a passage which really exemplifies the author and photocopy it for your class – this way it can be scribbled on and used as a writing prop by the children.

The True Story of the Three Little Pigs by Jon Scieszka inspired me on so many levels, but especially with the power of 180-degree writing – that is, writing from the completely alternative perspective, often in a very persuasive manner. It tells the story of the Three Little Pigs, but from the innocent wolf's point of view. It is hilarious, and really can divide a class with their opinions.

At its most simple level, examining traditional stories from the reverse perspective can open up fantastically rich conversations with the children, often challenging their ideas and beliefs and encouraging a more robust definition of their ideas as a result.

Taking it further

Encourage older children to choose individual books, type up their passage and the author's passage, and see if anyone can work out whose is whose!

The real benefit comes into play with junior-aged children, when you are able to ask them to respond to a passage from the polar opposite perspective, but in the writer's voice. This is a much more demanding task, but has enormous benefits in terms of making the children look at the content, perspective and writing style. This is best approached over a series of lessons, but the writing and understanding will really sparkle from the page.

#180degreewriting

Observation palettes

"Perfect for far more than simply nature walks."

A simple cardboard cut into the shape of an artist's palette, with colours and words on them, laminated, can provide so much use. These palettes take a while to make, but last for years and are worth the effort.

This idea came about on a class visit to an electricity substation, of all places. At the start of a nature trail, the leader gave out artist palettes with colours on one side and nature adjectives on the other. The children were told to see how many natural things they could match to their palettes. It gave an immediate focus to the walk, and the leader was able to stop and point things out when appropriate.

This is how you can pimp the idea! Using A5 coloured card, cut out as many artist palettes out as you need, with a few more for safekeeping. On one side, stick around six numbers, letters and colours, and on the other, around 15 different adjectives. This is done most easily by creating a grid of 100 different words (using different fonts), copying these six times, cutting them up and distributing them randomly.

Finally, laminate them and cut around the edges, leaving a 4mm laminated margin around the edge.

These are perfect for nature walks, but they can also be used to add spice to creative writing, to increase challenge for more able writers ('create a sentence/plot/story using three words from the palette'), they even work as conversation starters.

Teaching tip

Keep these in your Panic Tray (see idea 41) as inspiration banks.

Taking it further

If you are feeling brave, and trust your pupils with gluesticks, why not let them do the hard work and construct the palettes for you. The laminator may well have warmed up by the time this is complete...

Bonus idea ★

Encourage another class to make their own, then swap halfway through the year for some fresh ideas!

#observationpalettes

Bingo cards

"I laminated this. I'm a Primary teacher – it's what we do." @ICTmagic

There is, I believe, a feeling that bingo isn't a legitimate teaching tool, which I disagree with – used effectively and thoughtfully, it is a brilliant diagnostic and assessment tool which is front-loaded in terms of preparation. Create your own bingo cards and give your pupils Unifix cubes to use as counters.

My most-used bingo cards are those for units of measure and time numbers. I use the units of measure cards in a bingo-style game (thank you, Unifix cubes) at the beginning of a measuring unit to teach the concepts, during the week to revise and reinforce, and finally at the end as an assessment tool. They are brilliant for exploring and helping to build links between concepts.

The time number cards operate in a similar way. Each card has nine different time numbers (for example, 4, 60, 12, 1000, 24, 14) and I ask the class to cover up a number using a Unifix cube based on a statement or question, for example 'the word which means the same as 14 days'. I can see at glance who has understood the statement or question, and where I need to reinforce concepts. It takes ten minutes to play two games, and the children have to answer each question at pace, comparing against their own cards. I can make quick notes on a Post-it, and best of all – no marking!

Quick Unifix tip

Join all the Unifix cubes together into a larger cube of eight cubes. Keep them like this – it's not only easier to distribute and collect in this way, it neatly avoids the desire to have specific colour sets!

Some laminating tips

We are a profession of professional laminators. There are some teachers and schools where seemingly every single piece of work on display is flat, shiny and wipe-clean. There are others of us who find the wait for the wretched machine to warm up more painful, and so avoid laminating anything unless we have to. The range of resources I do laminate are also my mainstays. Some of these items are now over ten years old and still going strong, and my favourites are my bingo cards. Here are some tips from a laminating loather!

- Before you laminate, ask yourself why. To produce longevity of a resource is a legitimate reason. To make a display shinier is not the most productive, environmentally-friendly or financially sensible decision to make.
- If you are making small items to be laminated, give them a clear plastic border, or the plastic will peel off.
- If you are laminating something for display outside, any drawing pin or staple puncture through the plastic and paper will let water in and your work of (shiny) art will eventually be soggy. Trim the paper to size, keep the laminating sheet at full size and put any holes through the plastic, or, if you really need to use A4, use a hole punch on the corners of the paper before laminating, and you have a plastic-only attachment hole.
- Alcoholic screen wipes are really good for getting rid of any whiteboard pen marks.

You will find templates for the units of measure, time number and blank bingo cards in the online resources, expertly (flukily) designed so that Unifix cubes can be used as counters.

Taking it further

Laminators have vastly dropped in price in recent years – if you are allowed to, get one for your classroom and avoid the staffroom queues.

#bingocards

Vennspiration

"Of course Venn Diagrams and Carroll Diagrams are related – they have the same surname!" Henry, aged 8

Sometimes coming up with creative ideas can be a hard slog, with inspiration feeling like a dry tap. This method of generating ideas works brilliantly at encouraging random connections, building threads together and imagining new worlds in ways that remove the pressure and expectation of being 'creative'.

Teaching tip

Younger children might prefer to actually move the Post-its or have them on their tables when writing. Older children might need to be led to different choices, or given fewer (but more diverse) options.

Draw a very large Venn diagram on the board or screen. Decide on two very different categories – for example, characters and locations. This doesn't limit the imagination, but does refine choices. With a class of 30, it also doesn't matter if some children can't think of one for each, or even if there is some repetition.

Give out Post-it notes to the children, and ask them to write down something for each category and stick them in the right part of the diagram. Give gentle nudges to those children who are in mental lockdown! They can add something to either of the two zones shown.

Begin by modelling the process. Randomly select one item from each category and place these in the intersection. Start brainstorming with the class the story of why (for example) that character would be in the location.

Come up with lots of ideas, remembering that the most important principle of idea generation is not to reject any suggestions – this can inhibit some children from contributing.

Encourage the children to put two items together (mentally). If they can't think of a possible story, they can simply choose another two. With 30 suggestions on each side, there are 900 possibilities!

#vennspiration

Gritzones

"Stunningly simple and incredibly effective motivators."

Identifying the negative of a strength you wish to develop is an excellent way of motivating someone – for example, the opposite of productive is lazy! Using gritzones is a fun and fast way of helping children to stay focused and on task, with the addition of it being incredibly personal to them.

This idea is based on the Eisenhower matrix, but a much more simplified model. On a small piece of paper, draw a cross like a compass with an arrow each end. With the child in question, ask them a working quality they would like to have (speed, care, neatness, checking) and write this where North would be. Ask them what the absolute opposite of this would be, and write this in the South position.

Next, highlight and agree a quality you'd like them to work on, and write this in the East section, then decide on the opposite of this and put this in the West section.

Indicate the optimum learning zone (which should be the North-East area) and ask them to keep this diagram in mind. Tell them that all the time they have that diagram on their table, they are only working in one of the four zones. For example, if their two qualities are spelling and speed, then their optimum zone may even read "I am spelling well and working quickly" – it may help to write this in for some children.

This is a really simple system for keeping children focused and on task in a very non-threatening way, especially if you have made them part of the process.

Teaching tip

Share successful gritzones, or ask the children to randomly swap them for a twist on their normal focus.

Taking it further

Try this yourself – it really does work (especially for exercise and eating challenges!).

#gritzones

Conveyor-belt marking

"We read and helped with everyone else's writing!"

This idea works superbly for extended writing, but would lend itself to other types of work too.

Have the class sit in a big circle with lined books and ask them to write, on every other line, an extract based on the work you are carrying out at the time. Descriptions of settings or characters work especially well. Only allow 15 to 20 minutes for this; it should be a focused, intense writing period (I often use music for this type of situation – see Idea 78).

With the writing section finished, explain the following process. The children should pass their work clockwise, and they will be given one minute to read the extract in front of them and contribute (in coloured pencil/gel pen) one addition, spelling or suggestion. If they cannot think of anything to improve the extract, they put a comment on the writing at the bottom of the page. Once the minute is up, they pass the books clockwise once more.

This is an incredibly rewarding process. Not only are you exposing every child to everyone else's work, they are reading it for critique, and are actually keen to contribute too! The ground rules remain that you can accept or reject any changes, and that everything is a suggestion rather than a criticism.

This works especially successfully with draft work, allowing the children to reappraise their own work in light of the comments provided by the others. It will be the most-marked work your children will have in their books too!

Taking it further

If you can, join in too! Write at the same time as the children, and send your work around the loop. It's immensely satisfying for the children to mark the teacher's work, and you also get to see/mark everyone's extracts.

#conveyorbeltmarking

Class culture

Part 6

The long game

"Why won't you tell us what's in the case?"

The quick fix of daily lessons and inspiration is important and necessary, but the slow burn can also have an incredible impact on a class, if you are willing to play the long game.

Tony Jordan, the co-creator of EastEnders, once explained that a successful strategy of his scriptwriters was to sow seeds in the storyline – plots that grew over time. He recognised the slow burn was crucial in allowing the audience to form a bond with the story and characters. This is just as true in Primary classes.

Bring an old suitcase into school one day and leaving it at the front of the classroom. When the children see it, they will be immediately fascinated. 'What's in it? Open it!' Don't open it – the longer you refuse to open it, the more curious and keen they will be to find out what's inside. It's like a magician's trick – we want the illusion, not the boring explanation.

After a few weeks/months, use the suitcase for some creative writing. Introduce the Japanese concept of Wabi-Sabi, which, poorly translated, means the beauty of the imperfect. Show the children some pictures of crumbling old buildings and, together, write some descriptive writing based on the images. Explain that the suitcase had been found in one of them and ask the children to write a backstory about why it had been left there and by whom. Simply having the suitcase there will inspire the children – but you still shouldn't open it!

#thelonggame

Periodic values

"It became a ticklist of good values, with the children competing to be kinder, more thoughtful and more generous."

Using a blank periodic table to inspire good deeds can model kindness and thoughtfulness in an imaginative way.

The periodic table is an image that is instantly both familiar and alien. Its basic structure can be altered to suit any need – for example, qualities and demonstrations of values.

Templates are available online, and are easily expanded for any classroom display. Simply reproduce the chart on your classroom wall, then decide which values to highlight on each row – this can be done with your class. You might list on the side of each line, for example: thoughtfulness, sharing, honesty, generosity, gentleness, supportiveness.

Select a good deed and discuss where it might go on the chart. Decide first which row it should sit on, then talk about the value – is it a small act of generosity (near the left) or a large act (over to the right)? Summarise the deed or action in the periodic table style, so 'sharing my game' could become 'Sg', and then decide on a value – make this fun and arbitrary. Other examples include 'Writing a book review' (Br), 'helping with recycling' (Hr) or even 'Tidying the Teacher's desk (Tt)! Add items as the acts or deeds are carried out.

Once the children understand how they might get onto the periodic values chart, you'll be amazed at the industriousness of their thoughtfulness and kindness. What's more, your record of kindness and values is there for everyone to see, recognise and be inspired by.

Teaching tip

This idea will instantly give you 109 opportunities to build the classroom values and label them in a way which can be referred to and reflected on in months to come.

#periodicvalues

Registration inspiration

"I love registering, I always try to think of something unique to say!"

A legal necessity which occurs in those precious morning minutes, registration needn't be functional agony. Instead, try one of these quick tips for making registration a highlight rather than a scene from _Twilight_.

Drag and drop

This is a clever idea for those with a low-set interactive whiteboard. All the class have a photo on the board on one side of the screen, and register by dragging their face to the other side of the screen. The potential for mischief is high here, so a savvy teacher would also carry out a headcount as a safety net.

Numbers

For those with a particularly lively or large class (or even a lively large class), numbers work brilliantly as a speed exercise. Each pupil is given their registration number, and on the nod from the teacher, the children say their name aloud in succession. This is my mainstay on trips, and having the children lining up in this order removes some of the stresses related to out-of-school visits.

Hello to . . .

This idea is very similar to Numbers, except more friendly and personal (and a little slower). The teachers says 'good morning x', to the first person on the register. The first person then says 'good morning' to the next person, and so on until the last person says 'good morning' to the teacher. This is also good for encouraging eye contact and natural smiles.

Taking it further

Get more inspiration by speaking to your teaching colleagues about how they carry out registration. 90% will probably just say the names out loud, but you are after that elusive golden 10%!

Excuses

Great for a one-off, or even for a supply teacher standby, ask each child to come up with a farfetched excuse why they actually aren't there when you call out their names during registration. "I've been kidnapped by aliens" is a favourite!

Today's question

A favourite among smaller classes, Today's question is simple in concept, and incredibly effective in class bonding. The teacher sets a question, and the children have to answer. Where possible, try to encourage original answers, and don't let the squeaky wheels hog the limelight either! This is very good at encouraging fast thinking skills and responses, and can encourage the more reticent to speak up more often. For those who find the pressure of thinking on their seat too much, quietly tell them the question to them a few minutes before.

Here are some questions to use (note they get more personal as they proceed):

- Do you have any pets?
- What colour is your room?
- What is your favourite cereal?
- Where is the most beautiful place you've been to?
- Are you ticklish?
- What is your favourite smell?
- What height do you want to be as an adult?
- What was your last good dream about?
- How many people in this class know your middle name?

> **Bonus idea** ★
>
> Collate the questions you ask the children throughout the year in Today's question and you instantly have a ready-made set for the following year! If you keep a daily diary or day sheet, add these as you think of them to make life easier. I've even tweeted mine out occasionally to great responses!

#registrationinspiration

Ideal timetables

"We designed our own timetables, then voted for the best one."

The best way to empower pupils quickly is to let them take charge of their own curriculum — and a timetable is the silver bullet here.

The joy when children discover that they can dictate their own timetables can't really be surpassed. It is one of the strongest cheers you will hear!

Get a blank copy of your school timetable, with two copies for every child in your class. List the subjects you cover in one week on the board, and ask the children to redesign their timetable on the first sheet. Explain that each subject needs to be covered, but they can choose how much is needed in their ideal week! This creates a very rich conversation about the value of certain subjects, as well as the worth different children have for the subjects.

Now comes the magic: on the second sheet, ask them to design their perfect school week. They are allowed this time to build their own subjects in, provided they can justify their choices to others. This is incredibly exciting, and you will end up with a diverse range of weeks being planned — no wonder one size doesn't fit all, even at this age!

Taking it further

Be brave and take on some of their ideas if possible! For example, if the class is particularly keen on 'relaxation' as a feature before lunch then build in five minutes of quiet time — it will work wonders!

#idealtimetables

Classroom branding

"Finally, my classname has a meaning and a purpose!"

Building a class identity by branding it can make an enormous difference to your class purpose and morale.

It may seem trivial at first to have a class motto, phrase or slogan, but when the children support each other using that slogan, you can see the pride visibly in a way that no pep talk can ever hope to cover. Below are some ways in which you can brand your classroom. Use these to build an identity and make a clear stand for what being in your class represents.

Teaching tip

Carry these tasks out in the first few days of school for the ultimate bonding experience!

Motto/slogan

Why can't a class have a motto? This would be something you have over your door, repeat at key times, and, eventually, the power of habit lets the pupils take it with them as they move to another class. Younger classes tend to have this anyway, as they come home with phrases that are used a lot to ingrain positive learning and behaviour: 'What is sharing?' 'Sharing is caring!', 'What works?' 'Teamworks!' The easiest way to do this is to either borrow someone else's phrase or ask the children – they are never short of ideas! Class 4L could be Loving Living Learning Legends!

Logo

The logo can be as simple as the class name. If you have a shape, animal or bird, look up with the class what qualities this has. Have the children design a logo. Make those letters and numbers mean something. Even a 4 with a smile looks better than simply a 4. Go over the top and put the class logo on every exercise book and worksheet the children will love it.

Taking it further

Create a flag! This can accompany you everywhere you go when out of school, as it extolls the values you as a class stand for, and is great as a visual signpost when attached to a garden cane! Inspiration for the flags comes from the Bushcraft Company, who run brilliant outdoor survival residentials, and put the children into tribes (complete with flags, song and mythology) in the first few hours of any camp.

#classbrand

Good deeds

"The most fun you can have with kindness."

Perfect for an away day or a residential holiday, the good deeds activity never fails to bring out the best in everyone — adults included.

Teaching tip

Give some really simple examples of good deeds to get the ball rolling — carrying someone's bag, helping them over a stile or putting their lunch rubbish in the bin are all safe suggestions.

If you are ever away with a group of children, good deeds help to bond your group like no other activity, and, in addition, are an excellent midweek morale booster for when everyone is getting tired and antsy.

Put everybody's name into a hat, children and adults included. Mix them up and then sit everyone in a big circle and explain the rules. Everyone will pick a name and they will then have to carry out a kind gesture or good deed for that person in the following 24 hours. The aim of the game is to not get caught carrying out the good deed! The only really successful way to do this, is to carry out a range of good deeds. Explain that at the same time tomorrow you will regroup and see if anyone can guess who carried out their good deed. It is also really important that they don't tell anyone else who they have, no matter how big the temptation.

What normally happens next is a day of niceness, with everyone being overly kind to everyone else to throw them off the scent! If this doesn't happen, encourage a few of the adults to go overboard in helpfulness — the message and concept will soon spread!

Taking it further

I can still recall good deeds from years ago — test your class at the end of the year. Can they recall theirs?

By far the best part of this activity is the moment you regroup 24 hours later and go around the circle, with each person trying to guess who carried out their good deed.

#gooddeeds

Surreptitious signposts

"A daily reminder that they are valued, loved and capable."

Overtly giving praise has a place, but sneaky messages of affirmation can be both reassuring and encouraging at opportunities you might not have normally predicted. These aren't chances to demonstrate pithy sayings to the children, more to embed a strong and valuable class culture with the children which drip feeds support.

Name labels

The price of clothing and possession name labels just keeps getting cheaper, especially at a popular online auction site. For a few pounds, you can have a surreptitious signpost ('This is my best', 'failure isn't fatal', 'ambition is thoughtful') to attach to lent stationery, furniture, class possessions, bookshelves – anywhere it will get exposure!

Stickers

Similarly, stickers are still popular with children (even Year 6, given the right context). Stickers are best used as a reward for responding to teacher feedback, as this encourages thinking beyond simply completing the work well, and remember to use your sticker to praise the effort, not work!

Child swaps

For a low-cost alternative, give out a set of books to the wrong children and ask them to read through the pages and write a comment (in a coloured pen or pencil) of praise somewhere in the book. This little hidden nugget is incredibly rewarding, and will be looked at more than anything we teachers write!

Teaching tip

Download health and safety signs from the frankly brilliant and creative Sparky Teaching website: www. sparkyteaching.com. Hidden in these signs are messages and affirmations that, when discovered, make teachers and children smile.

Taking it further

Don't avoid ambitious language at any age. Two year olds can name and understand quite complex dinosaur names with ease. 'Optimism' for example, can be used when explained, modelled and understood; 'I'd love to hear an eight year old use optimism quite ordinarily in a sentence!'

#signposts

Choose your voice

"I never considered the impact and influence my voice could have."

Your poor children have to listen to your voice for hours every day – no wonder they are climbing the walls on Friday afternoon while you dream of that first glass of wine! Your voice is one of the most powerful tools in your arsenal, yet we're often guilty of not fully exploiting its potential (in fact, we tend to abuse our voices by straining them). Here are some tips to try.

When explaining something, try using 'mute' mode. This works especially well for expositions on formal maths methods. Model several times then switch to mute mode, and have the children guide you. The children tend to start talking to each other and challenging each other in a way they wouldn't normally.

Various studies suggest that teachers tend to answer two thirds of their own questions. Nearly everyone will be guilty of this – it's almost irresistible! Try instead to not answer any of your own questions, and create a system of fines, which the class know about, to help you with this (press-ups make a good forfeit).

If the children are getting louder, resist all urges to match them or raise your voice. The two most powerful things to get silence back is either to turn the lights off (which needs a little training but is an excellent quick fix) or to speak to a few children near you at a normal volume and gradually make your voice quieter and quieter. This has a magical effect and can even silence a school assembly.

Teaching tip

Suffer from regular sore throats? I do, and the best tip I have ever heard was for a teacher to imagine that there is a lit candle one inch from their mouth, and to speak in a way which wouldn't blow the candle out. Try it – this really works!

Taking it further

Change your tone, volume, accent or pace. Explore what is possible – teachers tend to speak faster with topics they are less sure of, so try to slow down at these points!

#voicetips

In our time

"I loved it when we used my clock for the day."

Our children spend a lot of their day at school. Why not let them have ownership of some of those hours? This activity fits in perfectly with any junior lesson focusing on time, takes little preparation, and rewards your class for several weeks.

Mark out the 12 sections of a clockface on as many paper plates as you have children in your class (plus a few more for spares). Make these simple markings, with enough space for numbers, pictures and details.

Discuss with the children the hours they spend at school, and talk about which picture or logo they could use to represent the hour numbers (feet walking for 8, mouths singing for 9, and so on). Ask the children to illustrate their clock numbers on their plates. Some children might want to characterise the numbers themselves, rather than use pictures.

Next, consider the fractional space between the hours – what could this time signify? Some children may want to dedicate each hour to something, while others may group the twelfths together. Encourage the children to illustrate these hours boldly and clearly. A particular favourite is the child who simply declared the morning 'Happy time' and the afternoon 'Smiling time' – what a brilliant rule to live time by!

Collect up all the clocks and, cannibalising the hand operator from a working clock, each day turn one of the class clocks into the 'clock of the day' – and don't forget to acknowledge the different times indicated!

Clock hand parts can be bought inexpensively from www.clockparts.co.uk

Taking it further

Allow the children to take these home at the end of the year – I'm reliably informed that some I have made with previous classes are still up at home seven years later!

#inourtime

Learning lanyards

"I love wearing my lanyard and visitors always ask me about it."

The rise in school security has also seen a growth in identity cards and lanyards, yet this hasn't had any impact on children's identities in class. This is a missed opportunity that the idea below hopes to address.

Teaching tip

Lanyards can be used to incentivise a class into striving to achieve one, can help bolster a more anxious but capable child, or can be used simply to publicly recognise achievement.

The charm of the lanyard to a child is great, and yet it seems only the important adults wear them. Now is the time to reverse this!

Choose some simple roles which are worth shouting about, and create grandiose job titles for them — Expert Speller of Complex Words, Genius Idea Generator, Razorsharp Problem Solver — and print these onto A7 cards, the size that fits into the lanyard pockets your kindly secretary has squirrelled away for you (or that you have bought on the internet).

At an appropriate moment, issue someone with a lanyard. This can be done with a blaze of public glory, but the system works excellently with children who don't like a lot of attention, so you may choose instead to give it to them privately. Nine times out of ten, you will see this child walk away from you bursting with pride and quietly sharing all who ask them what their lanyard represents.

The lanyard gives children a very quick status which is visible (from the band), focused (from the title) and temporary. Don't let just the adults have the glory of a lanyard; let the children have them too!

#learninglanyards

Presentation

Part 7

Underground maps

"It's great to see ideas I came up with connecting with other people's ideas."

The iconic London Underground map remains almost exactly the same design as when it was first created. In design terms it is both functional and quite beautiful, and lends itself perfectly to connecting ideas together.

Taking it further

Randomly divide up the stations and assign them to members of your class, letting them decide on the most appropriate word.

Bonus idea ★

Theme your Underground map and make it about your class, school or community. For example, each class could have their own 'line', and the whole school helps to identify children, deeds or tasks worth celebrating.

This idea is a simple – each line name is replaced by a word type (noun, verb, adjective, pronoun), and each station is replaced by a word suitable for that word category. From an educational perspective, it's fascinating to see how the different routes interact with each other, and to see several ideas converging to encourage wider word use in the classroom.

The challenge is deciding which words to include, and which words you can use on the intersections where two word types collide? This is the beginning of a deep and highly challenging activity played out over several days or weeks, with no right answer, which encourages a large amount of dictionary work, debate, research and conversation.

How you decide your best 11 adjectives to use on the (what was) District Line is best left to you and the dynamic you have created in your classroom. What is left, when you eventually complete your Underground map, is a testament to the legacy of words in your classroom.

The Underground map itself is protected by copyright. There are several homages, however, which are effective workarounds. Several are collected here: www.steveprentice.net/tube/TfLSillyMaps.

#undergroundmaps

Real-life graphs

"Graphs and charts in 3D give ten times the value of 2D graphs on the page."

There is so much rich and exciting stuff to measure and turn into graphs, but we can often fall into the trap of using materials such as coloured cubes. Capture the children's imagination and make graphs really easy to understand by creating real-life graphs. It allows the relationship between the tangible and intangible to form directly.

Height bar chart

Line up four or five children, of varying heights if possible, against a wall or whiteboard, and put a Post-it note adjacent to the tops of their heads. Step away, and you immediately have a real-life bar chart of their heights! Children can do the same with their fingers, coloured pencils (smallest bar = most popular colour), or even the heights of the water left in their flasks.

Pie chart

Using a camera or visualiser, cut a pie up! This can also be done with some generous donations of cupcakes and knives, ideally of different varieties so the children can swap halves or thirds.

Sunflower growth chart

This is great way to illustrate line-graphs. Plant a sunflower seed in a tall thin pot, and sit it on a windowsill on the left-hand side. Each day, have the children measure its height, marking this as a dot on the window using a whiteboard pen. Every evening, move the pot toward the right 2cms. In two weeks, you'll have a fantastic and quite genuine line graph!

Teaching tip

If you try a couple of these ideas, pool the pupils for suggestions of their own. You'll be amazed by what you get back!

Taking it further

Ask a handy member of staff or parent to cut some clear tubing (available from DIY warehouses) into equal lengths. Sat next to each other and upright, these are perfect for instant living bar charts for cubes. Or try using Lego blocks or even sweets!

#reallifegraphs

Hackasaurus rex

"This is the best introduction to coding ever!"

The software company Firefox has a little app called Hackasaurus (latterly, X-ray Goggles, found at goggles.webmaker.org) which is enormous fun to use. Although it has been designed to help lift the lid off the mystery behind coding, it in fact has far more use in the Primary classroom as a way of generating exciting and inspiring ideas and concepts.

The Hackasaurus app allows you to click on a section of a website and edit it. Imagine you have the BBC News page on your screen – you can click on the headline, the article, even the picture, and change it for something else. This is done by showing you the code, but it really is quite simple to edit the text or add a picture.

Use this to quickly create a writing stimulus or generate a challenge which has more authenticity than simply creating a 'spoof' news story in Word or copying something from a book. There is something really effective about using a familiar visual environment; you certainly get a better 'buy-in' from the pupils.

I have used this several times – once using a fake news story for an English stimulus, another time to help the children realise that they can't believe everything they read online. I've even adjusted a Sports page to convince the school secretary that her beloved Andy Murray had won a tennis match! This veers into the realms of practical jokes, which is absolutely what you should use Hackasaurus for after hours!

Taking it further

Let the children take over a web page and complete their writing tasks on the selected page. If you are planning to do this, have the children type up their story first, then cut and paste onto the web page.

#hackasaurus

Focus strips

"These work like a carrot rather than a stick for pupils and teachers."

Using strips within books makes tracking and concentrated tasks work far more smoothly – they are simple to use and adapt too!

How many good ideas appear from frustration in the classroom? This idea came from exactly that, when, despite several approaches, the class simply could not grasp the rules for starting a new paragraph. They knew the layout conventions to a fault, just not when to use them.

Use five simple prompts to remind the children when they could start a new paragraph (English purists, look away now):

- speaker
- place
- action
- time
- scene.

Print these onto coloured paper strips the width of a ruler, the five words repeating down the strip, and stick them into the children's books. You'll find that the difference this makes is incredible – the simple prompt down the entire page gives a gentle encouragement for the entire task.

The advantage of using coloured paper over plain white is that it is different in the short term, but also in the long term – when children flick back through their books, those small prompts return to remind the children again.

Teaching tip

Share focus strips online using a resource website on Twitter – you'd be amazed at the warm response you'll get!

Taking it further

Model more complex mathematical concepts like column subtraction using a focus strip as a handy and colourful aide-memoire for the children.

#focusstrips

Punctuation repair kit

"Brilliant – the novelty aspect caught their attention quickly."

Why rely on the children to supply punctuation when you can give it to them in the comfort of their pencil cases. This idea tells you how!

This idea was created as a name first, concept after, by a fastidious punctuation shield bearer (and the best teacher I have ever had the pleasure of working alongside) Sally Rose. We noticed that children regularly forgot their punctuation and would add it in afterwards – was there a way of reminding them about commas, apostrophes and speech marks so they wouldn't forget?

The punctuation repair kit was born. A simple template can be found in the online resources. It is simply a set of punctuation which fits onto a page of printed sticky labels. Print, then cut out one set and give them to your children to keep in their pencil cases. Tell them that they can cut out and stick the punctuation in whenever they get a chance.

You will discover an outpouring of punctuation. The novelty will soon wear off, but the recognition about punctuation won't. It will encourage a focus which was previously missing, or at least not the top priority. Keeping the stickers in the pencil case also means that they remain at the forefront of the pupil's minds (hopefully!).

#punctuationrepairkit

Anchor charts

"Personal and challenging – the learning equivalent of an in-joke."

Anchor charts are not my idea at all, but something I have made for years without knowing their name (thank you, Pinterest!). They are simply posters of review notes (summaries of a topic or learning theme), made by the teacher or class, and filled with a great deal of personality.

You can buy posters to help learning, but these are by nature quite generic and don't have the little phrases and lines you use with your class to embed ideas and concepts.

Make anchor charts with your class during a topic or at the end of a topic. Limit yourself to a maximum of 50 words, and make the poster simple, pictorial and as relevant to your class as possible.

For example, one year, the near-sound of Apostrophe and 'A Posh Trophy' appeared in my head, and our anchor chart was a giant and hideously ornate trophy, filled with apostrophe examples. This was highly personalised, so the central joke would have been lost on anyone else (indeed it was!), but for that class it made complete sense and they loved it.

Anchor charts make excellent revision and reminder prompts, but also help the children to think about the topics they have covered with you in a way which is tailor made. There is still a place for generic learning posters, especially if they have a blank back!

Taking it further

Ask the children to create their own versions from your design as prompts for their books, or invent their own from scratch as an end-of-unit assessment task.

Bonus idea ★

Use the children's anchor charts as decoration for the school, and share what you've been learning!

#anchorcharts

Hidden poetry

"Poetry should be treasured, and this way, it really is!"

Try this little idea for locating poetry in unusual places and watch the audience of that poem increase dramatically!

Taking it further

Take photos of all the poems in situ as a record, and use this as the basis of a class assembly – the charm is it can be at any time after you have put the poems up! You could even challenge the children to see if they can find all the hidden poems for a World Book Day activity.

There is a myriad of poetry out there to be discovered, but you often have to either read poetry books to find it or see it serendipitously. This idea works brilliantly for allowing your school community to discover poems hidden around the school grounds.

Start by discussing the sort of places the children might normally see poems. Where would they not see poems? Why is that? Take them to an area of the school that might not normally see poetry – this could be the space left when the dining room tables are out, or at the bottom of the register tray, or on the skirting board by the Head's office.

Write a poem there and then for that space (mini whiteboards may help here!) and stick it in place. Encourage the children to do the same – some of them will really love the 'sneakiness' of writing a poem that could be discovered at some point in the future.

Bonus idea ★

To earn huge brownie points with your colleagues, give the name of each adult in your school to your class, and challenge them to write a poem for them. Warning: there will be tears!

There are other children who may want to miniaturise their poem – this is to be encouraged, if only to imagine the Head on their hands and knees, staring intently at the tiny writing on the skirting board! Allowing the children a freedom to present their work is liberating for some, and can encourage greater creativity.

#hiddenpoetry

Word walls

"A near instant display, and highly interactive for all too!"

There is no chance of me describing this display as simply a giant Scrabble board using words instead of letters and Post-its instead of tiles. Oh, apparently I just did.

Cover a display board in light green board paper. Measure the width of a square Post-it and some masking tape, and use masking tape to create a square grid in the centre of the board using these measurements. This can be tricky, so now is the time to ask the brilliant arty TA, which every school has by law, to help you out. Try to have an odd number of columns/ rows if you can.

Fill the centre square with a large star, and give other squares random features such as 'three syllables' or 'double meaning'.

To complete the task, give each child a square Post-it, and ask them to write down one word which would match the theme (adverbs, angry adjectives, superlatives). Choose one to put in the middle, then ask the children to decide if their word could in any way connect to that first word. They'll become incredibly creative at this point! Allow them to build only horizontally or vertically, and only placing words next to related words (the relating aspect can become quite tenuous with younger classes).

Taking it further

When your class have finished their Post-its, leave some blanks on the side. It's lovely to watch this simple display grow over time, and the connections children make are fantastic!

#wordwalls

Myseum

"It made me really think about what was important to me, and what I wanted to share with others."

This concept is simple yet rewarding in the way that it encourages critical reflection, examines presentation skills and also allows your class to explain themselves through objects and memories.

Teaching tip

Exhibit the items interestingly, perhaps creating a tour guide of the items, or even a museum narration. Document the class finds too – a simple photograph and half-page summary put into a hardback scrapbook will be a gift for future generations, as well as a permanent reminder of your Myseum.

There was a BBC radio series a few years ago with an intriguing premise – the history of the world in 100 objects. How could you sum up all civilisation, changes, culture, architecture and habitats of our world in just 100 objects? What would you include, what would you (perhaps more importantly) exclude?

The Myseum grew both from this and from a pupil who found a small diary in the attic. We set up a small shelf, called the Myseum – the Museum of Me – a collection of items which the children felt represented them.

To run this in your classroom, ask the children to bring in five items (or photographs of their items) which most represent their lives. Alternatively, ask them to bring in three secretly, so everyone can try and identify whose items are whose.

Older children enjoy the challenge of researching old or unusual objects, artefacts that need to be explored through sight, touch, even smell!

Display the items on flat spaces or shelves around the class and have the children create small explanation boxes explaining why the items are so important to them.

#myseum

Flight procedures

"Everyone from the new child to the TA knows exactly what we do, and what is expected."

Having your class systems visible for all automates processes and makes your expectations clear, saving time and leading to smoother teaching.

There are many systems and procedures in our classrooms which develop, evolve or are set in stone. Have you ever stepped back and examined them? These 'flight procedures' are fascinating, and you should regularly re-examine them to ensure you am getting the most teaching time and least admin time.

Consider giving out or collecting in books. Who gets them? How are they distributed? Is there a more efficient way? Rather than every child searching for their book, could they each get a book and deliver it? Explore all options – you may find something which makes a real difference to your class.

Create the process in a visual format. The quickest way is to use images – preferably photos of the children carrying out the procedure. This way you are really embedding the system, and have a clear set of instructions for the children to follow, model and not stray from. Rules shouldn't be restrictions, they should be safety blankets, guiding posts, reassuring messages. Make one and see the difference it makes – 30 seconds saved in a day is worth 80 minutes of teaching a year!

For the skilled computer user, go to blog. spoongraphics and search 'safety instruction' for details on how to make realistic flight procedure cards.

Teaching tip

Display these flight procedures prominently, so visitors to your room can see how you carry things out in class.

Bonus idea ★

Do you have a new child joining your class? Why not ask your existing children to make a welcome pack for them, complete with one page summaries, flight procedures and some assorted top tips too?

#flightprocedures

Classroom set-up

Part 8

The tissue is the issue

"It seems so obvious now!"

It seems subtle, but where you place items in the classroom can have a huge impact on all aspects of learning and routine.

One common phrase in retail is that 'eyeline is buy line', meaning that what is visually available tends to sell best. Test this by looking at a typical supermarket shelf – the prices tend to grow with the height of the shelf, blending into specialisms at the top.

This transfers well into the Primary classroom. Try it with tissues: put two boxes in the class, one at the front and one to the side. Then see how long each box lasts. You'll find that the box on the side lasts several times longer than the stock at the front. Do the children really need to blow their noses, or is it the sight of the tissues that prompts them to get up?

This strategy works for a range of uses. Want to encourage ruler use? Make sure there are lots of rulers in front of the children. Are they wasting too much time drinking from their water bottles? Put the bottles on a tray behind the class. It seems obvious, but too often we automatically put the wrong things in the wrong places.

Take a class survey now. Sit in a pupil's chair, facing the way they'd normally face, and look at the message the front of your class is sending. What is shown? What is hidden? Now look behind you. What is hidden away that the class would benefit from?

#tissueissues

Class currencies

"One child's trash is another child's treasure."

One fact of Primary schools yet to be fully exploited is that whatever reward or point system operates in school, possession of Blu-Tack beats them all. This is the gold of the school currencies, but with careful thought you can build your own class currencies from the most innocuous of resources.

One currency I use in my classroom was born by accident from a method to help manage marking – keeping track by attaching a paperclip to the cover of the book that had just been marked. The children would keep the paperclips and started building them up along the tops of their books. Like that, a currency was born. All it took was two sentences:

'This lesson I'm going to be looking especially carefully at those writers who can use unusual adjectives in their writing. Two paperclips for those who really nail this.'

Cue a much richer set of writing experiences, all for some stationery! When some children get wise and start bringing in their own paperclips (smart!), you can order some coloured paperclips (smarter).

A class favourite was the Ludo-style counters and a pack of 500 lasts years. You can buy them now – they are called Halma Pawns: www.p4g.co.uk/en/en_prod_playpiece.asp

Another good and inexpensive currency which can be used are the bookmark-style Post-it strips, which I have found in pound shops. These are highly visible, easy to distribute and easy for the children to collect in one place too should you wish them to.

Teaching tip

The key here is how your currency is used. Giving out your currency sparingly, and accompanied by the qualifying value, is important. As one Head was fond of saying 'if the planes are all first class, it isn't really first class, is it?' Giving everyone a sticker devalues the purpose.

Bonus idea ★

Explore the actual values of some currencies in maths. How many Lego heads is a 30g ball of Blu-Tack worth? What about compared to a gel pen?

#classcurrencies

Classroom MOT

"A quick way to check your classroom's design."

So much is tacit about a classroom that sometimes it can be hard to see what could be improved or changed – this form helps you out.

This simple checklist was created from an awareness that there is so much to take in about classroom design – not what it looks like, necessarily, but what it feels like – that a prompt could help.

For example, despite being left-handed myself, I regularly forget that you are best to place a left-handed pupil on the left of a desk, to avoid elbow wars with the righty next to them.

Here is the classroom MOT in summary. Just before each half term, try running through this list and seeing how your classroom measures up.

- **Lights**: Are they all working? Are they above the desks? Any flickering bulbs? Any sources of natural light? Where do shadows form?
- **Sound**: What ambient sound is there in your class, and can it be changed? What furniture or equipment makes a noise which could be reduced?
- **Doorways**: Is your classroom clearly labelled? Does it have your class list, timetable and teacher name on it? Is there a fire escape sign on the back? Are the windows in the door clear?
- **Tables**: Are these perpendicular to the teacher's desk? Do they all have best access to provisions and the teacher? Any wonky desks? Are they safe?
- **Walls**: Are the displays covered? Are the borders peeling or secure? Is there anything on the walls which is out of date, serves no purpose or is looking very tired?

- **Equipment**: Is essential equipment at the children's eyeline? Are non-essential items sidelined (see Idea 71 for more information on this)? What support tools are available? What is stored behind the pupils? Are trays clearly labelled?
- **Books**: Are books easily accessible? Are they labelled? Are the procedures for giving out and collecting in books visible and understood? Where do children's books get stored? Where do they hand them in? Where is the marking pile? Who files marked work? Where does paperwork live?
- **Litter**: How many bins are in the classroom? How many more could you accommodate? Do you recycle – if so, is it clear? Do you avoid sharpening corners? Where do you hide stuff? Can you declutter these areas?
- **Pupils**: Have you sat in a pupil's seat? What is the view like? Can they see the board? Can they see you? Where are the classroom blind spots? Where do they put their coats? Where do they put their bags? Where do they keep their PE kit/musical instrument/show and tell toy?
- **Legal:** Where are register forms kept? Are the fire doors visible, clear from hazards and signposted? Are sprinkler systems and sensors active? Are windows locked?

You can find the full checklist in the online resources.

Taking it further

What is missing from the checklist? Let us know! Contact me on twitter using @mrlockyer and don't forget the hashtag!

Bonus idea ★

Have the children create their own classroom checklist. What would they put on it? What do they see as the necessary priorities? You could even ask them to create a Learning MOT.

#classroomMOT

Smother displays

"All the boards are filled within the week, and the pressure is off!"

In those first few days of term or teaching practice, the pressure sits on every teacher to fill those blank walls as quickly as possible. If you haven't tried out a Calendisplay (Idea 76), you might want to try a smother display.

A smother display is a crowd-sourced and supplied display which takes next to no time to create and mount – an instant win in Primary world! Here are a few examples.

My future plan

Find a template of a rocket, arrow, firework or any other projecting object, and give it to the children, asking them to write down their future plan inside the template. Keeping it vague allows the children to be specific or general, so you could have one person put that they want to be a nurse, while another might put 'to be happy' – it really is up to them. Decorate if necessary and attach them to the wall, pointing to the title 'My Future Plan'.

Wonderwall

Print out a 'thought bubble' image on A5 paper, and give one to each class. Ask them what they wonder about – again, keeping this open means that they might put a long paragraph, or simply a question. Stick these up (cut out of course) around the 'I Wonder' title.

Adjective tree

A blue background, some chalk smudges for clouds, some thin branches and 30 paper leaves are all you need to make an adjective tree. The children have to think of the best adjective that describes them, then illustrate this on the leaves.

#smotherdisplays

Taking the detail from retail

"It makes shopping more interesting, and my classroom is buzzing!"

Today's retailers have refined the art of selling to us in the most simple and effective ways. This thought process can be adapted to 'selling' inquisitiveness and learning in the classroom too. Below are some methods to try out in class.

Staff picks

Waterstone's encourages its staff to write mini reviews of books they are reading and put these on display. It shows a more genuine and human review process, and helps sales. Display your favourite reads around the classroom or school – demonstrate that you are a reader too! Even better – have the children add their reviews to the shelves!

BOGOF

The classic special offer of Buy One Get One Free can be adapted to a multitude of uses. Ask children to sharpen two pencils rather than one at a time, for example. Another tip is for children to collect two books and deliver them, rather than searching for their own. It saves huge amounts of time! Double up to save!

Express checkouts/self serve

I hate trailing queues of children, so offer an express checkout if there is a queuing system: to my right for 'depth' help, and to my left for an express answer such as confirmation of a task, question, spelling or other 'two second' enquiry. Toilet requests are carried out using a hand signal (fist on head).

#retaildetail

Calendisplays

"Instant displays and stimulation."

Not everybody is a fan of classroom displays. Ideas don't always translate successfully onto the wall, they take up huge amounts of precious time when other, more beneficial, work could be prepared and some people struggle to see the actual point of them. This idea tackles the issue in one hit.

This neat solution was inspired by the January sales. Towards the end of the sales, especially in supermarkets and department stores, you can find the most incredible bargains: out-of-date calendars. These are often on sale for a tiny amount, and with careful selection you can pick up some stunning colour photographic images printed on glossy large paper for a few pounds.

Simply use a craft knife to cut off the binding and mount the images on a board or frieze and you have a quick and hugely effective set of images, not only to decorate your classroom, but also to have as instant stimulation for your class.

Another way to do this is to buy poster books from discount book retailers. They are only a few pounds, often have superb images and brighten up the greyest areas of your classroom in no time at all!

Teaching tip

If you are worried about the educational value of your images, simply come up with a question for each, type it into a cloud or bubble, print (laminate) then attach to the display.

Taking it further

One variation is to ask your next class to send you a postcard over the holidays. Print out a colour map of the UK/Europe/the World, and pin this to the middle of a display board. At the start of term, pin up all the postcards. Do this two years in a row and you'll have a bank of postcards to use, and a geography lesson into the bargain.

#calendisplays

Reduce lesson admin

"It takes hard work, but we are always purposefully busy."

It is incredibly easy to keep children busy, or occupied, or active in Primary. This doesn't always equate to active learning thought, as the following example demonstrates.

The teacher is teaching the concepts of tallying, bar graphs and also prediction when rolling two dice together. The children have drawn tallying charts, and now have to roll two dice together 100 times to create their data.

The difficulty with this apparently happy scene in the classroom is that the time the children spend rolling the dice does not progress their learning or understanding of the concepts. Think of these times as 'learning admin' – things that happen around (or which lead to) learning, but which aren't inherently learning processes themselves.

It is terribly easy to fall into the learning admin trap, but with a little thought it can be avoided. Fortunately, most teachers build 'learning admin' into their lessons without realising. If they are writing subtraction sums, for example, how much time is spent copying, and how much time actually subtracting?

Try testing out a time-work study. Track exactly what the children are doing every minute in one lesson. Your aim is to decrease admin time and increase learning time. An easy way to do this is to say to yourself constantly 'are the children doing or learning?'

Teaching tip

In the dice lesson, there are several alternatives to having the children roll. You can either supply a tally filled in, which saves time but avoids tallying practice, or the teacher can call out the numbers. Not a perfect solution, but twice as efficient as the children rolling dice and tallying!

Taking it further

Consider the most time-consuming admin task you carry out each week, seek out the teacher in your school who has mastered this, and find out what their secret is!

#learningadmin

Soundtrack your day

"Creating a class atmosphere has never been easier!"

Instrumental soundtracks and ambient music lend themselves well to building an interesting classroom atmosphere. Here are some ways to make soundtracks work for you.

Music selection

Certain film soundtracks suit certain tasks. Writing horror stories? *Moon* composer Clint Mansell's suspenseful music. Writing resolution stories? Use the *Gladiator* soundtrack. Music can create and sustain a mood, and improves creativity.

General lesson music

Play music at a very low level to encourage children to work more quietly. Never use music to drown out noise – gamify sound instead. The quieter the music, the quieter they will get.

Lesson jingles and catchphrases

There are many songs which lend themselves to the start or end of lessons. An enduring favourite is Elton John's 'Are You Ready for Lunch?' which helps the children line up quickly and gives their lungs an airing! Seek out songs unique to your class and make them your own.

Music for timing

Some teachers use songs for specific tasks such as tidying up or getting ready to go home. These are more effective than simply stating 'you have five minutes', and, played regularly, they give children a familiar hook and countdown timer to complete their tasks. The *Mission Impossible* theme tune is perfect for this!

#soundtrackyourday

Order the changing

"Changing the order has made me re-evaluate the importance and priorities I put on things."

The difference between efficiency and complacency can at times be very slight. Efficient systems are found or created, developed, and then lock into place. Automatic pilot doesn't account for the varying needs of each child, and one of the simplest ways to break out from this is to stop, take stock, and mix things up.

An example – there is always a lot of packing away to do in Primary schools, and it can be both at the end of the day and agonisingly slow at times. Try changing the order of events. Ask the children to stand up, tuck their chairs under, then, standing behind them, pack away. The difference will be incredible!

Examine the one lesson or routine which you feel is on automatic pilot. Break it down into steps – writing this down is good. Getting advice from another pair of eyes (your TA or a pupil) is even better. Look at each event in turn – what could you do to change it? How could you improve or refine it? Is there another way this particular event could be delivered?

Next, look at the order you do things. Could the order be changed or reversed? Could events be grouped together another way? Could the time of day be changed, or the day itself?

Finally, give yourself a measure to compare against – something to look at in retrospect. In my tidying example above, I looked at it from a time perspective, but you may want to improve teaching time, learning admin or spelling retention rates.

Taking it further

Don't forget to share any tips that you pick up along the way. The two minutes saved tidying saves ten minutes a week, which is six hours a year. Imagine sharing this tip – how many hours could you save your colleagues?

#lockdown

We have list off

"Small change, big impact"

The humble list can make an enormous difference to your class set-up. This idea illustrates how to use lists to solve those nagging problems which steal time or cause anxiety for your children.

Taking it further

Combine these with Idea 70, Flight procedures. Making a list can often help to kickstart a flight procedure in the first place!

Desk lists are fantastic for helping disorganised children regain control. Sellotape a Post-it to their desks on Monday, and add to it when necessary. On Friday, remove it, type it up clearly, print and laminate it, then stick it down. This list is particularly useful for children when getting ready to go home.

Wall lists are quick and simple checks for not only equipment but attitudes as well. They are good to have by the PE kits, as a reminder of what is needed, and also by the door to ensure any home equipment is taken home.

Hygiene lists are fun to make with the children and can have a genuine health impact – in medical studies, they have actually saved lives! Lists of what parts of the hand to wash to lists explaining how to use the toilet (maybe add the 'lid down' instruction here) all have benefits.

Bonus idea ★

For younger children, use pictures for quicker impact. This can also be beneficial to children with EAL or who find language work difficult. Creating their own pictures is a great activity to get buy-in too – avoid clipart if you can.

Bookmark lists always help with keeping children focused on the bare minimum requirements. These can be individualised, but even generic lists have a benefit.

In short, don't be frightened of lists; it is always good to have a guide nearby, and it also allows you to address any issues when they slide.

#makealist

999 lessons

Part 9

Scratch startups

"Like Young Enterprise on roller-skates, crashing into *The Apprentice*!"

Merge rapid thinking and prototyping with a finished product, in one day-long activity. In this idea, children come up with, and produce, an item of saleable quality in one day with no preparation!

Teaching tip

This is the perfect activity for before a school fair, and really allows imaginations to shine. Year 6 can successfully run their own stall, selling their own produce and tracking their finances as the day goes on.

Split the class into groups, and tell them they are startup businesses, charged with making something for sale by the end of the day. They will be given tasks to complete throughout the sessions, and will operate on Take (divide up the next problem into solvable chunks for everyone), Break (split up and work individually) and Shake (regroup, report back and work out everyone's next steps) principles. Keep the pace fast, fun and focused – a progress chart on the board lets everyone see what they are all up to!

Here are two nothing-to-something ideas that work perfectly for scratch startups.

- Seed money: The groups decide on a fruit or vegetable seed to sell, and they must design the seed packets and advertising to entice green-fingered customers! (Note: lunchtime provides an appropriate moment to dash to the nearest garden centre if required.)
- Self-raising toys: Stress balloons are easy to make (see the link below), and you can quickly create a production line – the trick is for the groups to decide what theme they will market their stress balloons as, and how much will they charge. Googly eyes optional!

Taking it further

Find out the sorts of things the children buy at fairs and backward-design the challenges. Ask them about the things they have purchased in the past which have been handmade (sweets/cakes/toys), and see if they can work out how easy it would be to mass-produce them for their own fair.

Instructions for making a balloon stress toy, from the fantastic Instructables website: www.instructables.com/id/Easy-flour-stress-ball/.

#scratchstartups

Capacity challenge

"Water riot!"

This activity takes a little preparation but is incredibly enjoyable in terms of the richness of conversation. Put simply, the children have to compare different capacities and predict how much is in each container.

Collect together 26 containers of varying shape and size, transparent where possible. Using sticky labels, put a different letter of the alphabet on each container, and line them up.

Take some measuring containers and fill with water and some food colouring so the water is very clear to see, then add either 100ml, 200ml, 300ml, 400ml or 500ml to each of the containers. Try to do this as precisely as possible. Print out enough of the worksheets (a template can be found in the online resources) for your group, plus a few more for safety!

Set out the containers around the classroom in a non-alphabetical order. Tell the children that they are to pick one container to start with, estimate how much is inside and write this down in the first column, then find the next container in their alphabet (so if they begin on F, their next container is G). Continue until they have seen every container.

When they have completed the first task, give them a measuring container and ask them to physically compare it against the alphabetical containers, filling in the second column – this makes a real difference!

The final column on the sheet is for the actual measurement. This is a great part of the lesson; it can either be done together as a class, or you can assign a container to be measured to each of the children.

Teaching tip

If you choose sturdy containers then the set will last for years, and it will be regularly cited as one of the most memorable maths lessons.

Taking it further

Estimating is notoriously difficult, even for adults. How could you extend this idea to length, depth or estimated numbers (for example, numbers in a crowd or seeds in a packet)?

1 to 30

"Lots of fun and yet remains challenging too."

This task is incredibly adaptable and encourages comparison and discernment from children.

This idea was born from a desire to encourage more accurate measuring and estimating skills, after several more conventional attempts had fallen flat.

Create a sheet with the numbers 1 to 30 spread out over two columns. The challenge is to complete the sheet with the given focus, finding one thing for each of the numbers. In the case of the measuring example (see worksheet in the online resources), children were asked to find something measuring 1cm, 2cm, right up to 30cm, and everything in between.

This task splits into two distinct phases. The first is where the sheet is easy to fill in, and there are a multitude of items to measure. What happens in the second phase is infinitely more powerful – when there are perhaps ten slots left to fill and suddenly the children have to be more judicious in their selections and choices. It is only now that the children really start thinking strategically, and the conversations you can be active in are rich and powerful. Avoid letting the children share their choices.

While this activity works well for the measuring task described above, it could also work well with: counting items; finding numerals around the school; sections of writing with that many words; countries with populations in millions.

#1to30

Photoshop scissors

"Computing unplugged."

This is an example of an activity which is not only fascinating to carry out, but also teaches key principles which the children can relate back to their own computer practices. In the example below, the children physically manipulate photos that they might normally have changed using a program such as Photoshop.

Using a collection of images (a good stock of appropriate magazines, newspapers and travel brochures help here), create an image which represents a common saying or phrase, using only scissors and glue, such as 'a rising tide lifts all boats'.

Once the children have made their image, try to get them to recreate it using a photo editor. It may help for them to note down the process they followed for the paper version in order to assist their digital version.

When setting this task using just a computer, the stages and processes can become complex and filled with opportunities for distraction. By physically creating an image, the children explore in real life the types of decisions they would have to make using a photo editing program, but in a far more tangible way.

This is a useful exercise for many things we do in computing lessons – what is the offline alternative? If we weren't able to use a slideshow program, how could we make a visual presentation?

By encouraging thoughtful reflection about why we are using technology, we are also encouraging a more robust decision-making process.

Chatterboxes

"The return of a classic toy!"

Chatterboxes are quick to make, easy to decorate, and, used wisely, will provide hours of stimulation for both the creator and those playing with them!

Teaching tip

There is a fascination with chatterboxes in miniature, but large ones (A2 paper squared) can help with initial instructions too.

Chatterboxes are simple paper foldables (see link below) which can be made in minutes from plain square paper (although coloured is obviously far better), and end up looking like a beak. A child puts a finger in each pocket, and then they can open and close the chatterbox according to a song rhyme or other method. The child they are playing with or against can choose an inner section, with an answer underneath.

These are brilliant in that they can be prepared beforehand very quickly, but the real strength is in having children prepare them together. They work incredibly well for memorising facts, so lend themselves well to times tables, but can also be used for answering questions ('What is the capital of . . . ?') or cloze procedure questions ('What is the prefix: -vade, -side, -hale').

Encouraging the children to create their own questions and answers reinforces that they have been learning, and can also demonstrate this to others. If all the class do this, the variety of chatterboxes you will have will be huge (potentially 240 different questions!).

Taking it further

You can use chatterboxes as an assessment task. Ask your class to prepare chatterboxes at the end of learning about something to teach next year's class.

Easy instructions for building chatterboxes can be found at: snapguide.com/guides/make-a-chatterbox/.

#chatterboxes

Snow business

"Never let a rare phenomenon pass you by." Dot d'Urban Jackson

Extremes of weather can do incredible things to schools, but very often the most exciting ones such as strong winds or snow can close them! For those schools which don't close during a heavy snowfall, use this as a fantastic opportunity to explore snow in all its forms by creating experiments.

Test out what happens when you put the following on snow, and theorise why it may react this way: salt, sand, hot water, cold water, food colouring.

Fill several identical containers evenly with snow, place them around the school and measure which ones stay as snow the longest. Why would this be?

Walk down to a less-populated area of the school playground or school field. See if you can spot any animal footprints. Which animals are they? How do you know? What do the prints tell you about that animal?

Investigate desire paths. These are paths which people naturally use to replace paths which have been built, and desire paths are really easy to spot in snowy conditions – in fact, Swedish universities wait for snowfall before they build the paths between buildings!

Tweet out what you are up to during snow days to inspire other teachers and classes!

Teaching tip

Take a clear container of snow, place it in a warm location, and set a webcam to take a photo every ten seconds. By the end of the day, you'll have a small video showing the melting process available for when you cover it in science!

Taking it further

The hashtag #uksnow is used for the nation to report snow condition, and has become part of a crowdsourced weather station!

#snowbusiness

At boiling point

"This was quick to set up and really interesting for all!"

From broken boilers to flooded bathrooms, schools can close for a huge range of reasons. Use this idea to turn a problem at school into an opportunity for learning on the fly.

If the clarion call has gone out that children need to be collected by lunchtime because the boiler has broken, exploit the time left to carry out a classic heating experiment; at the very least, it will distract the parents from their emergency childcare arrangements when they come to pick the children up!

Collect some identical containers around the size of a jam jar, and some long thermometers (or at least one). Explain that you are going to ask the children to help identify the best sources of insulation by building a protective layer around the containers, filling them with hot (but not boiling) water, then taking the temperature every 30 minutes. Explain that you have laid out resources for them to use, but they can speak to you if they have any other material choices.

Watching the children becoming enterprising in their choices is fantastically rewarding, and this is an activity high in participation and rich in learning opportunities too. Track the group ideas and results as they come in together, making predictions and theories on the fly. Challenge their assumptions, and consider ways in which the test might be flawed. Relate it to what is happening in the school itself.

Bonus idea ★

If you run out of steam with this idea (apologies for the pun), use the same containers the next day but this time fill them with ice and water, then make accurate predictions on which container will reach zero degrees first (or last).

Archivists

"Creativity works best with boundaries."

Any situation with a restriction can give a valuable opportunity to reassess and re-evaluate resources, surroundings and the environment. Have the children help you to file school life in an emergency lesson, and teach them powerful archive skills.

We are a profession of hoarders, holding on to items for the 'just in case' moments in our school year – our cupboards may as well have 'break glass in case of creativity' in front of them instead of doors!

Use an opportunity during the year to have your children become archivists. Here are some simple rules to follow:

- Broken: fix or throw.
- More than two years old: find a new home.
- Old but unused: give it to someone who will use it.
- Precious: take it home.

Have the children help you to develop these rules as you go if necessary! The most satisfying areas to archive are the art areas – collect up all the half-finished packs and tubes, and lay them out in front of the children. What could be created with all these spare resources?

Books are particularly held dear, but if they aren't opened for more than three years then set them free by giving them a new home.

Teaching tip

How can we model clean learning for our pupils if we hoard ourselves? Free your shelves and liberate your cupboards!

Taking it further

For a pro approach, in the holidays, lay out everything from one cupboard and then assign it one of four places: binned, refiled, returned or taken home. Take no prisoners!

Fail trail

"Seeing where I went wrong showed me how often I'd actually been right."

We often look at mistakes made in a little-by-little process in schools – but the chance to review previous work, especially focusing on what has gone wrong, can be, if done thoughtfully and sensitively, a valuable and worthwhile task for both the pupil and the teacher.

It is best to carry this out with one specific subject at a time, and don't call it a fail trail (unless your class are attuned to FAIL standing for First Attempt In Learning).

With the children, model how to build a tally chart of mistakes. Each time something appears which is wrong, make a mark to identify what type of mistake it is. Using their own books, allow them to look not only at the mistakes they have made which have been marked, but also what they view as an error or fault.

The children will start to see patterns emerge, such as far more spelling errors or punctuation mistakes. This information may well be new for them (or you) and it is really valuable to build in some time at the end of this fail trail to reflect on what they have discovered. It may be, for example, that the weak speller actually has more problems with underlining straight.

The most important overarching aspect of this task is that it should have a positive finishing impact for the children (and you) – they should complete the task aware that they have strengths in certain areas which they weren't aware of, and that they could give a greater focus to other areas.

#failtrail

Feather your nest

"If a cluttered desk is a sign of a cluttered mind, of what, then, is an empty desk a sign?" attributed to Albert Einstein

Even the most well-equipped school faces an ICT lesson with no internet connection from time to time. This is a great opportunity to tidy the desktop, explore the settings, and find out all the built-in features on your computer.

Have a clear out

It is never too early to teach basic housekeeping, and organising files and folders on the desktop will please you no end. This task allows you to help children differentiate between a program icon and a file or folder, but it is worth creating a 'bin' folder for any unwanted files, just in case!

Accessibility settings

These are often hidden away in the Control Panel, but some are incredibly useful for classes without any specific need. The 'contrast' setting, for example, makes the viewing screen much easier to see and less distracting for some children. Spend five minutes acquainting yourself with the settings first before unleashing the children, to avoid an upside down screen or extreme magnification.

Pimp that screen

If the children have personalised logins, demonstrate how to customise their desktop settings by changing the background, icon placement and sizes, even their login logo. These are very small details that make a massive difference to the children's experiences on the computers, and are worth spending a little time on. The selfie is, of course, the most popular login logo at the moment. Risk the children having some fun!

Bonus idea ★

Google Chrome has a huge number of customisation options – explore the Google Apps product for your school, it is free and gives you an enormous amount of flexibility with customisation.

Nextperiments

Part 10

Signs of life

"I have only made this letter longer because I have not had the time to make it shorter." Blaise Pascal

Editing and cropping are incredibly hard skills to develop, let alone master, but this idea is perfect for thoughtful and deliberate editing skills with a unique spin — four activities in one quick sheet!

Collect a range of one-page instructions for various tasks. If you can, find instructions which are a little flowery in their writing — recipes can be excellent sources!

The children will need a highlighter, a different-coloured felt pen, a coloured pencil and an ordinary pencil. Their challenge is to reduce the instructions according to the following key guidance:

- Highlighter: highlight only the words which aid the instructions.
- Coloured pencil: loop up to half of the key words in the instructions.
- Felt pen: underline a maximum three key words per sentence.
- Pencil: summarise the instructions in your own words.

This task is very easy to differentiate, and can be adapted any number of ways by changing the instruction types, expectations of tasks, even the minimum or maximum words. By redacting existing instructions, they have to think carefully and critically about every single word, as well as the meaning behind those words.

Taking it further

Save this year's responses and use them with future classes to expand the summaries the previous class had written.

#signsoflife

UnGoogleable

"Inventive questions and even more inventive research skills too."

Designing questions which can't be answered immediately, then trying to answer them, introduces levels of complexity which have a multitude of rewards.

Setting the challenge of designing ten questions which can't be answered by Google really sets the imagination on fire. For example, 'Can you teach a hippo to backflip?' – is the sort of question which has probably never been asked and is utter genius! (Thank you Emma, aged 8.)

This encourages thinking about what an actual question is. The questions you want to encourage the children to ask are ones which do have an answer, but haven't been answered yet.

The second stage of this task is to ask the children to select a few of the questions and attempt to answer them. This is the perfect opportunity to introduce provenance to your class (if you haven't yet!), and to underline the importance of thoughtful research and showing where you obtained your evidence.

A really easy way of doing this is using Google Docs. Accounts are free, and you can make a class account with shared logins (check your school's ICT policy on this first though). There is an option within Google Docs called Research, which brings up a mini-Google on the side, perfect for searching for possible answers and leads, and also allows the children (in one click) to add a page link or reference into their document! Perfect!

Teaching tip

The research for an answer works best as a diary entry, and it is worth modelling this first, as there may not be an answer, but the journey is what's really interesting. Demonstrating this is very important.

#ungoogleable

Prep plus

"The children's engagement is so much stronger now, and the work they produce is much more rewarding to see."

There can be few greater joys for a teacher, having taught a particular topic or lesson, than seeing a child bring in a mini project the next day, which they have created at home after being inspired. But how can you encourage this?

In order to develop this behaviour, two steps are necessary. The first is that lessons need to be inspiring! Done that? Good.

Step two is to indicate to the children what they could do to demonstrate their inspiration. Try this approach:

'We know that Vikings had to wear clothes which reflected their lifestyles, environment and surroundings. What do you think your homework could be?'

This immediately frees the children to think of how they might approach asking the group question, as well as allowing them to share ideas.

'These are all really good ideas. Is there any way we could combine them?'

By giving the children the encouragement to combine their ideas, they will naturally want to contribute more than the minimum amount. This is a psychological technique known as anchoring.

'So given all these great ideas, what do you think the minimum amount for homework could be if you were short on time?'

Putting the emphasis on time here removes any escape clause a child might try to use.

Taking it further

Maths lends itself well to prep plus, but takes a little more organisation. The simplest way to manage maths prep plus is through open questions and created investigations. Even better, have the children create questions and ask other children to answer them!

#prepplus

Jigsaw projects

"The long-lasting pleasure of a project, without the huge amount of time normally needed."

Many of us will remember projects featuring highly in our lives at Primary school, and it is sad that so many changes appear to have brought on their demise. The pleasure in building something raw and authentic with your class hasn't diminished, so jigsaw projects allow this pleasure to return whilst maintaining everything that is squeezed into today's curriculum.

Demonstrate different types of project page layout. Encourage the children to consider the layout, presentation types and the impact that it has on the reader. Look at some sample pages from topic-based books, and point out to the children the way in which the writing covers a small section of the topic.

Ask the children (perhaps over a series of homeworks) to create three or four separate project pages – as if they had been taken out of different books. Encourage them to really share their interests and expertise.

When all children have contributed, summarise their pages in two or three words and put this on Post-its or small cards. Lay these out (you may need a few tables) and let the children look carefully at all the titles. Start putting them together, using broad categories suggested by the children (if necessary, guided by you). After a while, you will find that almost all pages can sit comfortably into around six groups –which are your jigsaw projects.

Design a front cover, have the children work out the content order and bind all the pages together.

Taking it further

This task really helps encourage categorisation skills, but if your class might find this hard then recreate the sorting task by using some random topics on cards and help the children to put them into broad topic groupings.

#jigsawprojects

Unpick the everyday

"This project made us look at the things we normally ignore with new eyes."

We can be led to believing that all that matters is the curriculum, but, like many things, the topics not covered often tend to be more interesting and attractive. As a rolling project, why not explore the boring, mundane, everyday stuff that surrounds us yet remains unnoticed?

This was inspired by a challenge to carry out a class assembly on anything, with paperclip as inspiration! A little background research found that not only were paperclips used as a sign of solidarity during the war, but their original design has hardly changed despite several hundred attempts, and, in the right circumstances, they can be exchanged for a house!

This activity works best as a whole class project. Decide on a very bland and potentially boring theme, item or subject, and brainstorm with the children a whole range of questions for them to try and answer around this theme. Set them the challenge of trying to answer their questions, and model the exploration of initially answering a few of these questions in class.

It may be worth carrying out this task in class at first, but it lends itself well to a homework project. Define for parents the sort of thinking and work you are looking for, and avoid this being seen as onerous or simply a time-filling project. You are trying to develop the children's questioning and research skills, but also encourage them to look at their surroundings in a fresh light. We are surrounded by wonder – so much that some things get hidden.

Postcards to school

"Flipped learning, but with a really positive message."

One danger schools have is that they can be seen as silos for learning, and that any learning that happens outside isn't legitimate. The irony of this is that most learning that occurs outside school is born from genuine interest or passion, rather than enforced.

This homework task lasts a week, but can reveal aspects of your pupils you might not have normally seen.

Cut 30 A4 pieces of card into quarters (hello, A6!) and give these to the class. Task them with returning one postcard every day for four days (by hand, rather than posting them to you), sharing something they have learnt from home. This could be some trivia over the table, something from their hobby or after school club or even something they read from a (deep breath) book!

On the other side of the postcard, they can illustrate their learning. This task is deliberately loose, which also allows the children to build as the week goes on, using my beloved spindle theory (research shows that people become competitive when they see someone else's work). Each day, share and display these nuggets of homework with the class: 120 new facts shared in one week!

Taking it further

Take a photo of the outside of your school, blow this up on a colour photocopier and make this form part of a display entitled 'learning outside school'.

Under the same sky

"Finally, homework with a really interesting purpose."

If you are ever introduced as a teacher at a party (which, please note party hosts, is a *very* cruel thing to do), it doesn't take long before the conversation leads to long holidays, strikes or homework. I'm a much bigger fan of the slow-burn homework as opposed to the complete-in-one-night task, which sadly seems far more common. Perhaps worse still is the weekend homework, which seems to be designed to ruin all family plans!

This idea is based around measuring something really simple. This could be the number of vegetables eaten each night, the amount of rainfall each day, anything that is easy to measure over a long time. This encourages a regular habit of doing something focused, as well as revealing patterns over time.

The most rewarding of these is to track the phases of the moon. All sorts of incredible apps are now available which identify the stars above us, but the primitive eye can still observe and recall the shape of the moon night after night and can record it pictorially with ease.

Tied into work on the solar system, ancient beliefs, time and even 2D shape, this is a lovely experiment which is rich in conversation, as well as lasting 28 days! It also avoids parents phoning each other to clarify what to do, or last-minute panics the night before the homework is due. Teachers, let your parents have a break from the homework with this one!

Bonus idea ★

Why not track the moon during the day? It is possible to see it on most days if you know where you are looking, and confounds our belief that if the sun is out, you won't see the moon!

#underthesamesky

Prepitaphs

"Thoughtful, passionate – the whole family found it interesting."

Epitaphs can be a tricky subject to tackle with Primary-aged children, their very nature being related to death. Prepitaphs are another matter. These are optimistic predictions of the future, and work perfectly as an experiment.

Begin by asking the children to make a fair prediction for six months' time. What will be the same? What will be different? How might the children view the different parts of their lives in the future?

Explain that a prepitaph is an autobiographical perspective on their future life. They are to try and write about what will happen to them, in first person if possible.

Outline how they might write their prepitaphs. Some children may want to write it chronologically, and so might benefit from some significant age boundaries to write against. Other children might prefer to write to categories – in which case, give some sample categories such as home, family, hobbies, work, holidays.

Encourage this task to be reflective in a predictive sense! It is very easy to come up with pat answers for the future, but this task has much more value if the children base their future selves on their present personalities.

Above all, these should be a celebration of future lives. Ensure this message goes home with the work.

Taking it further

Take a copy of these and keep it for the children for the future. I have 100 envelopes in my loft waiting for when children from my previous school turn 18. I still haven't worked out how I can get the envelopes to them though!

#prepitaphs

On your punctuation marks, get set, go

"Please stop using so many exclamation marks in your work!!!"

It is relatively easy to invent a new word and meaning for that word, but punctuation? That requires real thought and care!

Punctuation has taken on new forms and usages today, and creating a new punctuation mark is a really interesting task for children.

Begin by looking at some of the examples from the link below. These should provide some useful inspiration. Have the children consider times when a specific mark would be useful in their writing, and what form that mark might take. Would it be a variation on an existing mark, or a combination of two marks together (the comma and exclamation for example), or even a whole new shape?

Ask the children to draw their mark, write what it is for and give some writing as an example of how the mark could be used. You will be really impressed by their creativity!

Display these new punctuation marks – is there a trend for a specific style? Is there a problem with writing which these marks solve in some way? Carrying this task out gives quite an interesting insight into how language is used (and perhaps misused) by your class, but it also raises the status and purpose of punctuation in our writing.

This post is a lovely summary of some invented or defunct punctuation marks: www.buzzfeed. com/expresident/13-punctuation-marks-that-you-never-knew-existed.

#punctuationmarks

All that glitters

"I wish there was no tomorrow because then you'd never leave."

What if education finished at age 11? This question was posed by Bruce Waelend in a 2014 blogpost and kept me thinking for days!

We have the most amazing opportunity to have a profound and deep impact on the children in our classes. Teaching is a calling and an honour, and we are in service to every single child we say hello to in the morning.

We have a duty to ensure their safety, teach them what is necessary and guide them morally, but more important than all that is to give these precious children the best year we can possibly manage, filled with memories, laughter, thoughtfulness, tenderness, music and glitter. Lots of glitter.

Make the memories of their year with you the heroes of your story. Create an anticipation from the class below, and allow your classroom to be respite for the class above. Allow your pupils' ideas to take centre stage. Encourage the word 'why' as endlessly as possible, and make every single child in your class have value and worth.

Demonstrate that you are always learning too — try new things, use a dictionary, read in front of them. Look them in the eyes and never lie to them. Apologise if you turn up to work in a mood, remember the names of their pets and compliment their new glasses/hairstyle/pencil cases.

Here is a link to Bruce's post, Question Five: www.htbruce.com/six-challenging-questions/

Teaching tip

Keep your door open — there is a wealth of undiscovered talent in the classrooms and corridors of your own school — let them explore!

Bonus idea ★

Link up with your Primary world outside, via Twitter, TeachMeets, SLTcamps or conferences. These are often free, or heavily subsidised, and you can meet the most inspiring people at events or online.

#goprimary